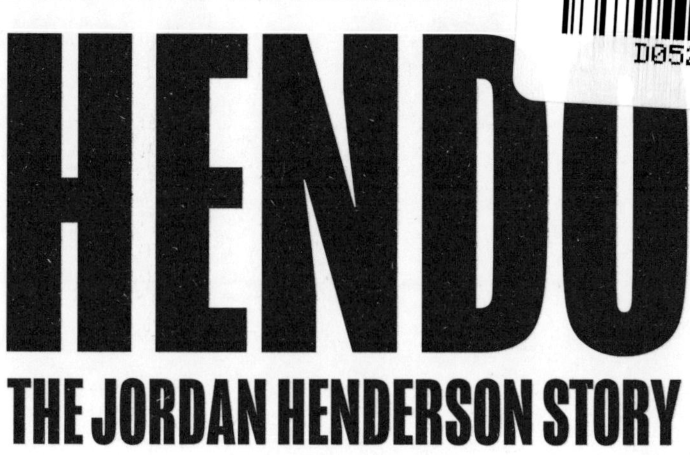


**by Rob Mason**

**G2** entertainment

**Published by G2 Entertainment Ltd**



**ISBN: 9781782817871**



**AUTHOR:** Rob Mason

**PUBLISHERS:** Edward Adams and Jules Gammond

**PICTURES:** Action Images, Press Association

**PRINTED IN EUROPE**

**THANKS TO:**

Jules Gammond, Steve Ogrizovic, Marcus Hall, Mark Hornby, Sarah Morris, Jim Brown, Kevin Ball, Ian Dipper and Scott Pearce.

# CONTENTS

Premier League
Premier League
Premier League
Premier League

# INTRODUCTION

From June 2019 to July 2020 Jordan Henderson captained Liverpool to the Champions League, UEFA Super Cup, FIFA Club World Cup and finally at long last for the Reds to the Premier League title. It was the first time Liverpool had been champions of England since they clinched the title in the season before Jordan was born in the summer of 1990, a time before the Premier League had even started.

Hendo: The Jordan Henderson story tells the story of a footballer who has achieved all this and more. In an era where so many players put themselves and not the team first Jordan Henderson stands out from the crowd by always putting the team before himself. So often criticised by supporters as he tried to achieve what Jurgen Klopp described as, 'the most difficult job in the last 500 years of football' by replacing Steven Gerrard, let Gerrard be the judge. Stevie G himself says of Hendo, "If I had to name someone I regard as the ultimate professional, then Jordan Henderson would come right at the top of the list. He is selfless, he puts himself at the back of the queue because he looks after everyone else first. He puts Jordan Henderson last."

'Hendo' traces the story of Jordan's rise to the top at Liverpool featuring his stints under King Kenny Dalglish who signed him, Brendan Rodgers who he had to win around but who appointed him captain and Jurgen Klopp who has made him a multiple winner. With contributions from people who coached him when he was as young as six, through his youth team years, early loan with Coventry City and rise to full England status with Sunderland this book follows the path of a player who has become admired and respected throughout the game.

Having followed Jordan's career since seeing him make his debut at Under 18 level he has always been someone I have seen invariably represent all that is good about football. During the coronavirus pandemic that cost so many people their lives and suspended the 2019-20 season, Jordan's initiative in bringing about the #PlayersTogether project illustrated that being the ultimate team player extended to warranting that accolade off the pitch as well as on it.

**Rob Mason**

July 2020

**Rob has written more than 50 football books, mostly on Sunderland but also on West Ham United, Burnley and Ipswich Town. He also produced 'From Zero to Hero' The Gareth Southgate Story, as well as Mirror Football's Ultimate Guide to the Premier League in 2020 and 2021.**

# CHAPTER ONE
# #PLAYERSTOGETHER

Positional strength is one of Jordan Henderson's greatest attributes. Not just with regard to his own position but his whole team's. Watch Hendo play and you will see that not only does he automatically cover for anyone who is drawn out of position but he'll direct others to do the same. This isn't simply a reactive response but a pro-active one. Henderson has long been adept at making runs that make space for team-mates to exploit. Rarely if ever does he get the credit for this unselfishness but in the case of #PlayersTogether it was there for all to witness.

As the nation pondered players on their PlayStations or counting their money during the Coronavirus Lockdown of the Spring of 2020 Henderson's hopes of imminently lifting the Premier League crown were put on hold while he dreamt up a scheme of organising Premier League players as a whole to do something positive in the face of awful adversity.

No one doubts that Premier League footballers earn vast amounts of money. Some ostentatiously flaunt their wealth but the vast majority do not, living quiet lives and trying to ensure that if they attract the attention of the press it is for the back pages and not the front. A stranger to the front pages of the national tabloids Jordan found himself there early in April 2020 not because of some misdemeanour or error of judgement but due to his leadership in contacting every other Premier League captain to forge a way forward for footballers to independently make a significant financial contribution to helping the National Health Service at a time when every doctor, nurse, hospital cleaner or other employee was waking up every day and knowing that when they went to work they were putting their own life at risk and with it the consequences for them and their families.

Suddenly the pressure that people talk about in sport seemed laughable. Playing football, golf, tennis or whatever your chosen game is after all a game. There may be high level stakes involving prestige, money or both but nothing to compare with thinking coming to the aid of stricken people could see you in serious danger yourself.

AFC Bournemouth captain Simon Francis was one of those to confirm that Henderson was the man behind the players' initiative. He told the BBC, "Jordan took the initiative to pitch the idea to the rest of the lads and it was a no-brainer for us." A player who made the journey from League One to the Premier League with the Cherries, Francis added, "It's a great chance for players to show how much the NHS means to us - a cause that is close to a lot of players' hearts." The Cherries skipper's view was backed up by his vice-captain Andrew Surman who added in the Bournemouth Daily Echo, "I have to take my hat off to Jordan Henderson for what he has done with the fund he has set up."

Conor Coady, the Wolves skipper was another to acknowledge Henderson's leadership, 'Jordan was brilliant in terms of setting up and taking the initiative and moving forward with it and then getting in contact with everybody. As soon as he did, everybody was on board straight away. So it's a brilliant, brilliant thing that he's set up and something that'll affect a lot of people"

Burnley captain Ben Mee first played against Henderson in 2008, contesting a two-legged FA Youth Cup semi-final in his days with Manchester City while Jordan was with Sunderland. The Clarets captain wrote in the Guardian, "Jordan Henderson might be the captain of the European champions but he is also a working-class lad from Sunderland who deserves full credit for bringing us all together, showing what makes a true leader. As a group we just wanted to do something positive, and we feel we have taken a step towards achieving it. From the moment Jordan called me, the Premier League captains have worked tirelessly to ensure we could get #PlayersTogether in place in such a short time. There has been great collective urgency to help in any way possible, while at the same time ensuring our funds are directed to the places that are most needed. Naturally, such a complex matter needs time to sort, but our frank discussions always had the same purpose: to help in any way we can."

Government Heath Secretary Matt Hancock had annoyed many when he said on 2 April 2020, "Given the sacrifices that many people are making, including some of my colleagues in the NHS who have made the ultimate sacrifice...I think the first thing that Premier League footballers can do is make a contribution, take a pay cut and play their part."

A self-claimed supporter of Newcastle United, Hancock's lack of knowledge of football was illustrated a couple of months later when he referred to Daniel Rashford rather than Marcus Rashford after the Manchester United striker's success in forcing a government U-turn on proving meal vouchers for under-privileged children.

Andros Townsend, Robert Snodgrass and Sam Allardyce were amongst those to criticise Hancock for targeting footballers, when in a government of millionaires, but Bournemouth's Simon Francis was quick to point out that Henderson had been working away quietly behind the scenes before the Health Secretary made his ill-judged comments, "I don't want it to seem like it was a knee-jerk reaction to what has been said in the media - it wasn't that at all. I spoke to Jordan in the morning of the day Matt Hancock came out and made his comments, so it was bad timing. With the problems we have across the country, for him to pick out footballers was disappointing."

Typically, reports in The Times spoke of Henderson not wanting to be credited with the initiative. Notably when #PlayersTogether announced themselves to the world with a statement it was unsigned by any individuals. This further strengthened the collective ownership of the project which reportedly would see the #PlayersTogether fund administered by Jordan along with the captains of Manchester United, Watford and West Ham: Harry Maguire, Troy Deeney and Mark Noble. These are some of the most highly respected men in the game. Maguire of course is an international team-mate of Henderson, and like Jordan, came to one of the country's most prominent clubs having started with his local team, in Maguire's case Sheffield United who were relegated to League One early in his career.

#PlayersTogether's announcement on 8 April 2020 stated that over the course of the past week a group of Premier League players had conducted numerous talks, 'With a vision of creating a contribution fund that can be used to distribute money to where it's most needed in this COVID 19 crisis; helping those fighting for us on the NHS frontline as well as other key areas of need. This is a critical time for our country and for our NHS, and we are determined to help in any way that we can."

The statement went on to confirm that after "extensive conversations between a huge number of players from all Premier League clubs we have created our own collective player initiative #PlayersTogether and have partnered with NHS Charities Together." Further, the announcement also made clear that #PlayersTogether was about players collaborating together to create a voluntary initiative, separate to any other club and league conversations, adding that their thoughts and prayers went out to everybody affected by the crisis. 'By sticking together, we will get through this' it added.

These words looked like the work of a professional PR company but the sentiments were genuine and that line about getting through this by sticking together was pure Hendo: looking for teamwork to produce a result.

Setting up such a group as #PlayersTogether was no simple task. Quite apart from the difficulties of getting in touch with everyone there was plenty to negotiate through a long series of individual and conference calls. Not everyone earns the same amount within one squad let alone 20 different ones at clubs of varying sizes and most people don't want to reveal what they earn. Being careful not to make some individuals look less generous than others was just one of the hurdles to overcome. With an initial aim of looking at players' take home pay for what should have been the last two months of the scheduled season in April and May a basis was laid via each club captain for players to donate a percentage of their monthly wage to the scheme with any additional donations warmly welcomed.

This was achieved in the face of some clubs looking for wage reductions from their players as clubs lost some of their revenue streams. Another factor to overcome was the wishes of players from overseas to see their contributions aid Covid 19 responses in their home countries.

Taking control of their own situation and making their own voluntary contributions to the fund enabled the footballers of the Premier League to do something positive in a situation where they were otherwise powerless but simultaneously to maintain control over how and where this money was spent rather than seeing it disappear into a fund administered by clubs or the league itself.

Match of the Day front-man Gary Lineker was amongst those quick to praise the scheme tweeting, "Footballers are doing their bit as I was confident they would. Let's hope that others that are in a position to help, those that weren't unfairly targeted, do likewise. Proud of our players." The top-scorer at the 1986 FIFA World Cup soon added a follow-up tweet having seen a large number of players swiftly show their support for #PlayersTogether via Instagram, Lineker saying, "Absolutely brilliant. Well played to each and every one of them. Young men setting the right example." Lineker, who captained England when winning 18 of his 80 caps then completed his hat-trick of tweets with "Great job" accompanied by three clapping emojis.

Former Liverpool striker Stan Collymore was amongst many others to voice their approval of the Anfield skipper for the lead role he had played in bringing his fellow professionals from all 20 top flight clubs together. Speaking to the Daily Mirror the ex-England international proposed that an MBE or OBE should be headed Hendo's way, saying, 'The conscience he has shown football these past couple of weeks is more important than any trophy he will ever lift for Liverpool. Henderson has been the driving force behind the #PlayersTogether campaign and no-one should under-estimate the work he will have had to put in. A few might say, 'What are you talking about Stan? It will only have meant him calling a few of his mates.' Yes he will have had a couple of numbers through England, but even in the best of times getting hold of the rest of them wouldn't have been easy. Don't under-estimate either how much work will have had to go into having chats with everyone and working out with 19 other fellas the mechanics of what you need to do and the right vehicle for the support you want to give. That isn't easy at all. Then you have to make sure the money gets to the right places - the NHS and other community initiatives set up to help people during the Coronavirus Pandemic – and again it's not something that's straightforward. The way Jordan has conducted himself has been exemplary."

Sure to become an outstanding pundit of the future because of his honesty in front of the camera, Watford's Troy Deeney backed up Collymore's assessment on Match of the Day X, "You're talking about getting every player from every Premier League team all on the same page, so it took a lot of work in between the captains and the players, but massive shout out to Jordan Henderson, he's done a lot of groundwork, him and James Milner. We've got a WhatsApp group with all the captains, so it's just a case of talking, 'what do you think about this? What do you think about that?' and it's everyone's input. We've all raised a huge sum of money and it's hopefully all going to the right people as well. It shines a good light on what football is really all about."

Like Henderson James Milner is another character who gives the lie to the stereotypical image of the spoilt brat footballer. "Jordan has done an incredible job" he noted. "I wouldn't like to see his phone bill and probably the stick he's had from his missus the amount of time he's been on the phone over the last few weeks."

It wasn't just players who were impressed. Fans' message board were full of compliments, especially those regarding His current and former clubs. On the Liverpool site 'We Climbed the Hill in Our Own Way' for instance 'Peabee' commented, "He's great. A massive heart and the motivation to do good off his own back. People will point out that they're wealthy but I don't see any billionaires going to this effort...While Hancock was having a go at rich 'working class' lads Henderson had already put this together.'

Meanwhile on Sunderland's 'Ready to Go' message board, 'Well done Jordan. Class', 'No words for this man can do him justice' and 'Not surprised. A great role model for kids and young players' were amongst the first comments to be made about Jordan after the announcement of #PlayersTogether.

Still failing to impress many football people both inside and outside the game, Health Secretary Hancock tweeted a positive response saying, "Warmly welcome this big-hearted decision from so many Premier League footballers to create #PlayersTogether to support NHS Charities. You are playing your part" but many felt he could and should instead have been directing his ire at tax-avoiding multinationals and perhaps some not a million miles away from his own government.

While #PlayersTogether earned a lot of media coverage it is far from the only thing Henderson has done to help others. The month before the announcement of #PlayersTogether Henry Winter revealed in The Times that with football suspended the matchday food collection points of Fans Supporting Foodbanks on Merseyside had taken a hit at which point Henderson had contacted local MP Ian Byrne to offer the support of Liverpool's players, "Jordan told me that he'd seen our appeal and the players wanted to help" revealed Mr. Byrne, "... the players have committed to covering all of the shortfalls that we will incur as a result of not being able to hold our usual match day collections."

Just as after striking a defence splitting pass Henderson doesn't stand there admiring it but stays on the move, after creating #PlayersTogether he was still looking to do more. By early May he was leading a drive to raise more cash for the NHS with a new scheme called #shirtsforheroes. This involved every first teamer from Premier League clubs signing a shirt and having them raffled on eBay.

Typically Jordan maintained a low profile despite playing the leading role in establishing #PlayersTogether, his aim being the fulfilment of a target not self-aggrandisement. As this book will make clear there cannot be a footballer who is more devoted to the game than Jordan Henderson. His initiative in creating #PlayersTogether to benefit the NHS at a time of genuine crisis illustrated that the Liverpool captain is a real leader whether on the pitch or not.

Jurgen Klopp is renowned for his touch-line passion. Usually a charming character off the pitch he metamorphosises into a whirling dervish dancing along the touchline in the heat of high-octane matches. Yet with his reigning European and World champions having nine games to secure the maximum two wins they would require to guarantee their first domestic league title since the month before Jordan Henderson was born, Klopp assumed statesman-like stature.

As football was suspended on 13 March 2020 at a time when ten deaths had been reported in the UK due to Covid 19 Liverpool's manager commented, "First and foremost, all of us have to do what we can to protect each other. In society I mean. This should be the case all the time in life, but in the moment I think it matters more than ever. I've said before that football always seems the most important of the least important things. Today football and football matches really aren't important at all. Of course we don't want to play in front of an empty stadium and we don't want games or competitions suspended, but if doing so helps one individual stay healthy – just one – we do it. No questions asked. If it's a choice between football and the good of wider society it's no contest. Really, it isn't."

Klopp's comments contrasted with Liverpool legend Bill Shankly's most famous quote, "Some people believe football is a matter of life and death. I am very disappointed with that attitude. I can assure you it is much, much more important than that." Always a man of the people, 'Shanks' may well have reconsidered this in the situation Liverpool leaders Klopp and Henderson were faced with early in

2020 but the actions of the pair demonstrated genuine class at a time when more than one representative of other Premier League clubs were issuing statements where the chief beneficiary was evidently their own club. Liverpool's craving for a first title since before the creation of the Premier League was well known but Klopp's concern for the public was genuine and Henderson's leadership in contacting every other Premier League captain to see what they could do to offer practical help was arguably more admirable that whatever he or anyone else for that matter has achieved or will achieve on a football pitch.

## CHAPTER TWO

# ALL THAT GLITTERS ISN'T GOLD

"He is the best midfielder in the world in his position" is not an opinion on Hendo even many ardent Koppites might venture. The statement came at the beginning of 2020 from Jorge Jesus, manager of Brazilian giants Flamengo, the 2019 Brazilian and Copa Libertadores champions and the man named Brazil's coach of the year for 2019. The former Benfica and Sporting Lisbon boss had just seen his side lose the FIFA Club World Cup final to Liverpool and had no doubt who was the key player, the man who makes Liverpool tick.

In the late sixties when Manchester United ruled Europe and had three of the world's best players in George Best, Bobby Charlton and Denis Law aficionados often reckoned the man who made United tick was midfielder Paddy Crerand. Many didn't realise how important Crerand was until he was missing. Crerand was a different player to Henderson, nowhere near as mobile or with the same stamina but he could pass, and like Hendo has a brain which is the football equivalent of Stephen Hawking.

Jesus is not the only person to rate Henderson as the world's best midfielder. A huge number of Liverpool's goals involve world class wing-backs Trent Alexander-Arnold and Andy Robertson. They both know how good Hendo is. Alexander-Arnold described Jordan as 'the best midfielder in the world' in an interview in January 2020 while three months later when Andy Robertson was asked whether Lionel Messi or Cristiano Ronaldo was the world's best player his instant answer was, "You heard Trent, Hendo."

Pundits picking the best 11 individuals in the world might not go for Henderson, perhaps picking instead players capable of more flashy moments that thrill YouTube viewers. Remembering that if you want great individuals tennis and golf are the sports for you, in a team game a player like Hendo with the mentality to always utilise his talents to the ultimate benefit of the side is a player who his team mates recognise the true worth of.

Dietmar Hamann and Steve Nicol are amongst the many other top professionals to understand exactly what Jordan contributes. Having won six major honours in his seven years as a holding midfielder at Anfield Hamann has an appreciation of a player who has shown he can excel in that number six role, as well as playing more expansively when asked to. "I remember when Henderson signed, he cost about £20m quid and I think a lot of people said he would never be a Liverpool player" said the former World Cup finalist. "Then he took on the captaincy which is not an easy thing because they are big boots to fill following Stevie as the captain of this club. So it just goes to show if you keep believing in yourself and stay determined what can be done. He has improved every week and season, he fully deserves all the accolades he is getting now. If you tell (sic) somebody after two seasons that he would have been a Champions League-winning captain, they would have said, 'Not in a million years'. But that shows the character of the player and man and you have to take your hat off to him for what he has done."

Steve Nicol won four league titles, three FA Cups and the European Cup with Liverpool. He too is massively impressed with what Henderson brings to the Reds. In May 2020 he told ESPN FC that Jordan had made a bigger impact on the club than the exceptionally highly regarded Xabi Alonso. "Well you have to say that Henderson's been more effective because Liverpool have won the Champions League and he's pushed them...As great a footballer as Alonso was, I think the influence that Henderson has had on this team has been bigger than Alonso had. Listen, as football players, Alonso's a better technician than Jordan Henderson. I don't think that's in question. So it becomes the biggest impact and I think no doubt Henderson's made a bigger impact in this Liverpool side than Alonso did for the team he played for."

Jake Livermore has never played for Liverpool although he sounds as if he should. Playing the game of building the ultimate player with 'The Athletic,' when considering the engine of a perfect player the West Brom midfielder had no doubt, "It has to be Jordan Henderson. He just doesn't stop. 'Energy' is the word that sums him up in terms of his work rate and resilience. I have played with him for England, but I've also played against him a lot and I've always noticed that he's very good in terms of energy and stamina."

Closer to home, another midfielder to recognise how Hendo helps his team above and beyond what some might appreciate is Georginio Wijnaldum, "I've played with a few players who have great leadership. I have to say, Kevin Strootman and Jordan Henderson were, I think, above the other ones" he told Sky Sports in May 2020. "Mark van Bommel was also a good leader and a good captain, but out of the three of them, I have to choose Henderson. It can be annoying [when he is cajoling teammates], but if you think about why he's doing it, it's only to help you as a person and the team. So if you think about it in that way, you always appreciate it, so we are really happy with the way Henderson is."

So how good is Jordan Henderson? Is he the world's best midfielder or should he not be a fixture in the Liverpool and England line-ups? Tony Cascarino says he isn't just Liverpool's player of their 2019-20 Premier League winning season but is in fact the Reds player of the decade. Speaking on Talksport the former Chelsea, Villa, Marseille and Republic of Ireland forward said of Hendo, "Okay he might not have been as good as Steven Gerrard. Luis Suarez had his brilliance for a year – two years probably. And you've had some great players play for the club; Salah has been brilliant for two years, like Mane, and there are a huge amount of players. But if you're talking about 2010 to 2020, Jordan Henderson has done nine years there and he has ended up being part of that side under every manager so I can't see how it can be anybody but Jordan Henderson."

Cascarino has a point about consistency. During the decade from 2010 to 2019 Jordan played in more Premier League games than any other player, his 308 appearances being two more than James Milner and Ben Foster.

Since joining Liverpool just before his 21st birthday in 2011 Henderson had ran his heart out for Dalglish, won over Rodgers and progressed under Klopp. However until the end of May 2019 a League Cup winner's medal won in his first season, and a batch of runners' up medals, were meagre reward at a club like Liverpool used to glittering success.

All that changed on June 1st 2019 when Jordan captained his club to Champions League success. This was followed up within a few months by the addition of the UEFA Super Cup and that FIFA Club World Cup where he so impressed Jorge Jesus, but for many the Holy Grail was still to be found. Liverpool were league champions when Hendo was born in 1990, having lifted the title under the man who signed him, King Kenny Dalglish. They had never won it since, never having got their hands on the coveted Premier League trophy, something not achieved throughout the era Liverpool were led by the iconic Gerrard. Had it not been for the coronavirus crisis that closed down sport in the spring of 2020 Hendo's side would have claimed the Premier League long before 25 June when they finally did so. Raising the top domestic trophy to add to the clean sweep of major European and World honours was the climax of a dream year in which Jordan was named BBC Sport Player of the Year long before the season ended, with the likelihood that come the end of the campaign there would be further honours to follow.

In a unique season where the final stages were carried out before a world watching only on TV and not in the ground, Liverpool's title was finally sealed without them even playing. Twenty four hours after demolishing Crystal Palace 4-0 the squad gathered to watch Manchester City fail to win at Chelsea, thereby guaranteeing what had been all but a mathematical certainty for ages: that is that Jordan Henderson had become the first ever man to captain Liverpool to the Premier League title. It capped a golden 389 days that begin with Hendo raising the Champions League trophy. "To finally get over the line is a relief but also an amazing feeling. It's a unique feeling and one that I'm very proud of." Hendo told his club's website. "I've been so honoured to be part of this football club right from the first moment that I came and to go on the journey to be with this manager, this group of players, these fans - it's been so special."

Everyone likes a winner. With Liverpool filling their trophy cabinet once again boundless praise has come the captain's way but the contribution of a player who has always concentrated on getting the job done for the team and not hogging the headlines as an individual has not changed. It is simply the perception of him in some people's eyes that has. Henderson has always merited the recognition he is now getting in the reflection of the glory of those trophies he has raised.

It wasn't just Jordan's trophy cabinet that was being filled. Nine months after the sensational Champions League comeback against Barcelona his wife gave birth to a son, a brother to their two young daughters.

The maturity that comes with being a father of three children as well as a devoted son became better known to the wider world when the tragic consequences of the Coronavirus pandemic led to Jordan becoming more of a national figure. Suddenly he wasn't simply a trophy winning Liverpool captain – there have been lots of them – but a person who featured on the news pages as well as the back pages. A clean living lad, focussed on football and family rather than frivolity Hendo had to this point been a stranger to the non-football pages of the papers – except for those that wanted to send paparazzi photographers to snap Hendo and his wife on holiday beaches. There was an attempt to turn a November 2016 trip to a Bournemouth lap-dancing bar with Adam Lallana on their day off from England duty into a minor scandal. For the tee-total Henderson this was a one-off out of character story that was blown out of all proportion.

In April 2020 Hendo appeared on the news pages, not due to stories of a non-drinker possibly drinking but because of the way he took his leadership role beyond the football stage to the national stage. Jordan did this by leading his fellow professionals from across the Premier League to significantly contribute financial support to the fight against the virus.

By this stage Henderson commanded the utmost respect from his fellow professionals. He had always had this due to his selfless and consistent displays for club and country, but by now looked up to as the captain of the European champions he had undoubtedly gone up a level in the eyes of the wider footballing world.

A year on from beating Tottenham 2-0 in the Champions League final in Madrid Jordan reflected on the experience in an in-depth interview with liverpoolfc.com, "[It was] every emotion you can think of really. Joy, relief, happiness, just everything that you could possibly think of." Speaking of the moment Damir Skomina's whistle blew for full-time at the Wanda Metropolitano Stadium he recollected, "It was just the most special moment to hear that final whistle go, to know that all of the hard work and everything that we have done together in the past however many years, we actually got over the line and managed to win one of the greatest trophies ever. It was everything I dreamt of and more really."

Like Liverpool, Champions League final opponents Tottenham Hotspur had made a fantastic recovery at the semi-final stage. In Spurs case, having lost the first leg at home to a young vibrant Ajax looking to revive their great days as a continental powerhouse, the Londoners went to Amsterdam, conceded early and found themselves 3-0 down on aggregate at half-time in the second leg. Mirroring Gini Wijnaldum's quickfire double of the previous evening against Barcelona Lucas Moura scored twice in quick-succession in the second half to bring Spurs right back into the tie. Just as the former Feyenoord and PSV player Wijnaldum felt he was destined to face a team from his homeland in the final Moura struck a hat-trick goal that – due to away goals counting double – transformed defeat into victory six minutes into added time.

Liverpool had done the double over Spurs in the Premier League, but so had Manchester City who Tottenham had knocked out of the Champions League. Nothing could be taken for granted. Anyone who knows anything about football knows that is a fool's game at any level, let alone the top level. Liverpool had the advantage of most of the team having played in the final a year earlier and a history of being European royalty, but for all their past success in the Cup Winners' Cup and UEFA Cup this was Tottenham's first try at a Champions League or European Cup final. "A lot of us had been there the year before and experienced that and I think it did help us come the second time around" explained Hendo. "Just that experience, game-management stuff within the game, how you would feel prior to the game and the adrenaline and stuff like that. I think once you've experienced it then the second time around you can learn a lot from that, and I felt as though we did that."

Spurs had shown against Ajax, and also against Manchester City, their ability to come from behind in big European games so Liverpool taking a second minute lead via a Mo Salah penalty was welcome but far from conclusive. It led to a very different Liverpool performance from the swashbuckling extravaganza which had thrilled the global audience for the semi-final second leg against Barca. Considering the way his side managed the final in which that slender single goal advantage was held for 85 minutes Hendo explained, "It maybe changes the mindset a little bit for both teams, but ultimately I thought having scored so early on, having reflected on the game and watched it back - because when you are in the game and are trying to find solutions straight after the game you think we didn't quite play probably to the levels that we had previously and wasn't a great performance. But actually when I analysed the game and I looked back at it I thought we handled the situation very well. It was a very mature performance, we defended really well and did everything we needed to do in a final to win the game, so there was still a lot of positive things looking back.

"One-nil is a dangerous score-line because one mistake or one special moment from a Spurs player and it's all level again. It's always dangerous but in the best way I thought we controlled it defensively really well. We are known a lot for going forward, creating so many chances and scoring so many goals, but I thought the defensive performance from everybody that night was pretty good. Even though we were defending for maybe large parts of the game I still felt in control. We did it very well and we were hard to break down. I knew if we could create one or two more chances going forward then we can get another one."

Another one did of course come three minutes from time, Divock Origi adding to his semi-final heroics to seal the deal and leave Jordan Henderson the skipper of a team making Liverpool European champions for a sixth time – a feat bettered only by Real Madrid and A.C. Milan.

As Liverpool lifted the Champions League trophy, amidst the outpouring of emotion and joy there was a moment that surpassed even the heights you might expect of such a triumph. Jordan has always been close to his dad Brian. A former police officer who played football for England police, Brian Henderson has followed his son's career extremely closely since Jordan was six. It's one thing proudly watching your son from the posh seats at Champions League finals and World Cup semi-finals but this is a man who watched game after game in the wind and rain at pitches where there was no shelter at all from the biting North Sea wind as Jordan played junior football. Five years before the magical moment of Champions League glory in Madrid Brian had had to tell his son that he had cancer of the throat. "Before that happened I thought getting criticism and things like that was difficult but that was the most difficult time of my life. I wasn't prepared for that day." Jordan later revealed.

After a lifetime of knowing his dad was watching from the side-lines suddenly Hendo went into his games without his father being there. Dad had to restrict his viewing to watching on television having insisted Jordan didn't see him after his first round of treatment – something so unselfish and indicative of where Jordan gets that trait from. "He wouldn't let me [see him]. He's a very proud man and he didn't want me to see him because of how he looked. I knew the only thing I could do, the only way I could help him, was to play well on the weekend because I knew he'd be watching. That's a different pressure. I wanted to play well to help my dad be healthy again."

A highly respected individual on Wearside where he still lives, Brian ran a double-glazing company after leaving the police and thankfully came through his battle with cancer and is well again. Lifting the Champions League trophy a year after captaining Liverpool as they lost in the final to Real Madrid was a career peak for Jordan. He had given a lifetime's dedication to reach that moment, but beyond even that, the on pitch embrace with his dad was one that the viewing TV audience knew should have been private but were compelled to watch. It was a moment more beautiful than the match, a moment of sheer love between father and son.

Later Jordan revealed, "It was just something that happened. Would I have preferred the cameras not to be there? Probably, so you couldn't see us crying! But that's what football's all about - the emotion, the passion that I have for football and that my dad's had over the years. With what he's gone through for me to get where I am, and how much it means to him, to then see him such a short time after the final whistle was an amazing moment and one that I'll never forget." Of course it was not only his dad Jordan shared the joy of winning with. Reflecting on how special lifting the Champions League with he later added, "It was very special. Not only my dad but my mum as well, my wife, my family being there obviously means a lot. But, especially my dad after what he'd been through over a long time really, a few years leading up to it, and how much it means to me to be able to win that trophy and everything that we went through together. To be able to spend that moment with him so quickly after doing it was a real special and unique moment."

After winning the Champions League there was still one gigantic goal Liverpool wanted. Having been league champions in over half of the last 20 seasons before the start of the Premier League Liverpool had never won the Premier League itself after 27 attempts to do so.

The Reds had gone so close to winning the Premier League along with the

Champions League. Liverpool accumulated 97 points, more than any team had previously achieved without winning the title, but one short of champions Manchester City. Liverpool had topped the table for 141 days, 16 more than City, without being there when it mattered. As European champions in 2019-20 they simply steamrollered their way to the Premier League title, brushing all before them to one side and collecting the UEFA Super Cup and FIFA World Club Cup along the way.

After holding domestic treble champions Manchester City at Wembley only to lose the Community Shield on penalties, the season started with a 4-1 thumping of championship champions Norwich City before Hendo lifted the UEFA Super Cup. This time it was Liverpool's turn to win on penalties, beating Chelsea after a 2-2 draw in Istanbul.

By the time Jordan started two high scoring European Championship Wembley wins for England over Bulgaria and Kosovo in September Liverpool were two points clear of defending champions City. This came on the back of a 100% record from the first four games, Hendo having played in three of them.

Although there was a surprise 2-0 loss in the Champions League away to Napoli – who had beaten Liverpool 3-0 in Edinburgh in pre-season – the Red tide in the Premier League moved on relentlessly. By the time Hendo was picking up yellows in England's October trips to the Czech Republic and Bulgaria – the latter a game shamed by racist incidents – a huge gap of eight points had been opened up at the top of the table as Liverpool maintained maximum points from eight games.

That 100% record was dented next time out in Manchester, but at United rather than City as a 1-1 draw was played out at Old Trafford. Just possibly the title charge could have been damaged further had Liverpool not immediately returned to winning ways. Following a mid-week Champions League win at Genk (Where Hendo was rested as an unused sub), Harry Kane gave Spurs a first minute lead at Anfield the following weekend. It was a challenge Liverpool had to overcome if they wanted to show their title credentials were genuine. Spurs almost doubled their lead when Son hit the bar after going around keeper Alisson shortly before Hendo got his side back onto level terms, coming in on the far post to score with his left foot. Salah went on to complete the job with a winner from the penalty spot.

By now Liverpool seemed unstoppable in the Premier League. Losing 1-0 at Villa with three minutes to go Andy Robertson had no time to celebrate when he equalised, instead racing back for the restart. That paid off as Sadio Mane hit the winner from a trademark near post corner routine deep into injury time. They weren't just gegenpressing in games, Liverpool seemed to be gegenpressing between games because of the pressure they were putting on City and any other title aspirants. As City came to Anfield – Champions League progress having continued with another win over Genk in midweek – Pep Guardiola's men were already staring down the barrel of a nine point gap should they be defeated. Bernado Silva had scored late on when City pulled back from 4-1 to 4-3 a couple of seasons earlier and his goal 12 minutes before time on this occasion was a mere consolation. Liverpool had led 2-0 inside quarter of an hour and 3-0 after another goal early in the second half. Mane headed home a sumptuous Henderson cross from near the corner flag after a bullet from Fabinho and a header from Salah had set Klopp's contingent on their way.

By Christmas Liverpool held a 10 point lead with a game in hand ahead of second placed City, but leading the chasing pack were not Manchester City but Brendan Rodgers' Leicester City who Liverpool were due to visit on Boxing Day. Liverpool arrived at the Kingpower Stadium as newly crowned world champions.

Two tight games in Qatar had seen Bobby Firmino score winners in games against Mexican champions Monterrey and then in extra-time against Jorge Jesus' Flamengo. Demands on Liverpool were so high at this point that Klopp left Neil Critchley in charge of a very young side who were beaten 5-0 at Aston Villa in the Carabao (League) Cup 24 hours before the Monterrey game in which Henderson was employed at centre-back. The Mexican side caused a few more problems than might have been expected, having eight efforts on target. Suffice to say Jorge Jesus would not have thought Hendo was the world's best centre back (That was Van Dijk, who was ill) but once again Jordan's willingness to do whatever he could to help the team was self-evident.

The final saw him twice go close to helping Liverpool take the lead before his raking 40 yard ball to Mane opened up the Brazilian defence for Firmino to open the scoring. Earlier Hendo had set Firmino up only for him to hit the post and then Jordan himself had been foiled by a terrific save from Diego Alves after a measured curling shot from 23 yards.

With the Club World Cup keeping the European Super Cup and the Champions League trophy company in the Anfield trophy room there was still one gaping hole the club wanted filling and the challenge to fill that gap would continue at Leicester.

Rodgers' Foxes were unbeaten at home where they had conceded just five goals in nine games but they were simply swept aside to the tune of 4-0 on their own patch. Three goals in a devastating spell three-quarters of the way through a pulsating game ridiculed any idea that Liverpool may have been exhausted by their trip to the Middle East.

Following the handsome win at Leicester Liverpool went on to win the next nine Premier League games, a sequence that extended the run of successive Premier League victories to18. Hendo controlled the midfield in the first eight of the nine following the Leicester game, scoring one and making one in another 4-0 win over Southampton. During this run Jordan sat out the cup games which saw a youthful Liverpool knock Everton and Shrewsbury out of the FA Cup, the Shrews only tamed after a replay.

Of far bigger importance to Klopp was the Champions League Round of 16 meeting with Atletico Madrid, the first leg taking Liverpool back to the Wanda Metropolitano where Spurs had been beaten just over nine months earlier. Whereas Liverpool scored early in the final they trailed early against Atletico, Saul Niguez netting in only the fourth minute. Against a renowned defence Liverpool had 72% possession but could find no way through, Henderson heading their best chance wide in the 74th minute. Six minutes later there was worse news for Hendo as his hamstring went.

Consequently Liverpool went into their next game with West Ham minus their captain, having to come from behind to beat David Moyes' struggling side with a late winner from Sadio Mane. A 26th Premier League win of the season meant that as the end of February approached Liverpool had astonishingly only that October draw at Old Trafford impinging on an incredible 100% record. Defending champions Manchester City languished an amazing 22 points behind with Rodgers' Leicester by now a further seven points adrift. Liverpool were just three points short of having double the number of points of fifth placed Manchester United.

This had all been achieved on the back of unrelenting desire which showed itself in the ability to grind out win after win even on the days when the football wouldn't flow and teams weren't blown away early on.

Next up was a trip to second bottom Watford. The Hornets had been stirred by the arrival of former Leicester boss Nigel Pearson but as they welcomed the champions elect were without a win in six, a run that included FA Cup elimination at Tranmere Rovers. Victory for the visitors was expected at Vicarage Road, even by most home supporters. Had it come Liverpool would have set a new record for the longest winning run in the top flight in England. It would be simplistic to say that Liverpool's shock 3-0 loss was purely down to the absence of their captain, but on a day when the league leaders were sloppy with the 70% plus possession they had it is undeniable that had Hendo been on the pitch his ability to drive the team on would have made it much more likely that Liverpool would not lose. This was especially the case in the manner of the defeat, conceding three goals in 18 second half minutes after struggling with the high press Watford employed. It was a case of the biter bitten as Liverpool were beaten in the Premier League for the first time in 44 games, stretching back to defeat at Manchester City over a year earlier. Without Hendo Liverpool had conceded two or more goals in back to back Premier League games for the first time since 2016, conceding more in the two post Atletico games without him as they had in the previous 14 Premier outings. The mentality monsters had missed the biggest mentality monster of all.

The 'Rousing the Kop' website was one of the places that recognised this. Headlining an article, 'Watford defeat typified why Jordan Henderson has become irreplaceable for Liverpool' it talked of Henderson silencing his army of doubters and stated that without Hendo, "Liverpool lacked their usual drive, control and energy from midfield. Far too many second balls were lost. There wasn't a commanding presence. His imminent return cannot come soon enough." Similarly Paul Clarke, the Liverpool Echo's Senior Sports Wire Writer noted shortly afterwards, "Henderson has been the engine that's allowed the Reds take a 25-point lead at the top of the Premier League. His importance was arguably seen most of all during Liverpool's loss to Watford without him."

Jordan was also missing as a mix and match line-up went out of the FA Cup at Chelsea and he continued to be absent as struggling AFC Bournemouth were edged past by the odd goal in three at Anfield. Having missed four games since being injured in the first leg against Atletico the medical team had worked wonders to get the skipper on the pitch for the second leg on 11 March.

As some three thousand Atletico fans enjoyed the bars and cafes of Merseyside the UK was reporting 86 new cases of Covid 19, bringing the country's total to 456. Two new deaths from the disease were revealed, bringing the UK total to eight. In Spain 54 deaths had been confirmed from 2,231 cases. The decision to let the game go ahead would become a topic of a debate more serious even than Liverpool being deposed as champions of Europe. Over 90 minutes a goal from Gini Wijnaldum squared the tie at 1-1 and when Firmino's first home goal of the season put Klopp's men 2-1 ahead on aggregate four minutes into extra time it looked as if Diego Simeone's side's famed defence would not be enough to stop the Red tide.

Just as Loris Karius' blunders had cost Liverpool the trophy in the 2018 final to Atletico's rivals Real, this time Adrian – filling in for the injured Alisson – dropped a clanger. His poor clearance gave Marcos Llorente the chance to not only score but provide the side with the iron defence a crucial away goal. The same player stuck a dagger into Liverpool hopes with another to make it 2-3 on aggregate on the stroke of half-time in extra-time. After playing 105 minutes on his comeback from his hamstring problem Hendo was replaced as Liverpool looked for fresh legs but with Jan Oblak superb in the visitors' goal there was no way back for a team needing two goals in 15 minutes against a side they had scored against twice in over 200 minutes. When former Chelsea man Alvaro Morata scored in the last minute to give Atletico victory on the night as well as on aggregate it was a huge disappointment but one tempered by the imminent sealing of the long awaited Premier League title. "Tonight and tomorrow it'll not feel nice but we've got to use it and react in the right way and finish off the season well." Jordan told BT Sport immediately afterwards when as usual he was looking to the future rather than the past. "We've got the derby next, which is a big game for us. That's what the focus has got to turn to very quickly because that's a big game and [we'll] just keep taking it game by game until the end of the season. We want to finish it strongly."

Little did Jordan or anyone else know it would be over 100 days until that derby with Everton could be played and when it was eventually staged it was at a time when Hendo would have been planning to be in the thick of Euro 2020 action with

England. Between the game with Atletico and the match at Everton more people had died of coronavirus in the UK than could fill Goodison Park. A most sobering thought that puts football into focus.

As football was suspended with no-one knowing how the season would be completed, or even if it would be at all, numerous personalities rushed to offer their opinions. Oddly enough these opinions concerning how the season might end – such as by making it null and void – tended to correspond with what would benefit the clubs of the speakers. With Liverpool on the verge of mathematically sealing the Premier League title they craved to Jurgen Klopp's immense credit he came out and said, "I don't think this is a moment where the thoughts of a football manager should be important, but I understand our supporters will want to hear from the team and I will front that." Going on to insist that regardless of how important football was the health of people had to come first Klopp spoke with warmth and humanity.

In the spell between the Atletico Madrid and Everton games when football and much of life came to a shudderingly unscheduled halt Hendo showed the same sort of leadership that Klopp demonstrated with those comments. Most especially his initiative in setting up the #PlayersTogether funding for the health service was outstanding but despite becoming a father for the third time during this period he continued to think of others.

Just a couple of weeks into what became the footballing desert of the spring of 2020 Jordan was telling his club website, " I think it is important to stay in touch with people, especially the lads. Some people cope differently to others. Some of the lads are on their own who I've spoken to, which must be really difficult. Most of the lads have family and kids and stuff, which will make it easier – maybe a little bit more difficult at times! But overall a lot easier when you've got family around you and people around you. But when you're on your own it must be so difficult, so I've touched base with those lads and they seem okay but it's only been a couple of weeks and we've probably got a few more months to go at least. Again, especially when you're from a different country, you might feel alone but the lads and the people at the club will make sure that they feel supported in everything that they do and the programmes and stuff."

A little over two weeks later on the 31st anniversary of the Hillsborough disaster Jordan was again thinking of the wider Liverpool and footballing family. He released a video saying, "Today was a day when as a club we were all supposed to be together at Anfield to honour the lives of 96 people who went to a football match and never came home. The fact that we are unable to do so will make this anniversary especially hard for the families and survivors of Hillsborough. I'm not one for making speeches, but on behalf of all the players at Liverpool I just want to let everyone affected know that you are in our thoughts today. As ever, we are together in spirit even if we can't be together in person. You'll never walk alone."

Liverpool had looked nailed on for the title. Deservedly so as they had destroyed all before them. Using the footballing mantra of taking one game at a time, Henderson had also destroyed any talk within the camp of the job being done before it was completed. As Alex Oxlade-Chamberlain informed the Liverpool Echo in March, "I look at Jordan Henderson because he's lifted the European Cup, how much that meant to him, but you wouldn't have thought he'd lifted anything from the way he is. If anyone even utters the words 'winning the league' then he shuts them straight down. He's done it externally as well, he won't ever let himself get carried away. He's just so driven, focused on the next game and the next thing."

When the Premier League did get going again, over three months later, Liverpool speedily completed the formality of mathematically confirming the result of a one-horse race. A goalless draw at Everton was followed by an outstanding 4-0 win over Crystal Palace before defeat for Manchester City at Chelsea confirmed Liverpool as Premier League champions. In the most hotly contested league in the world, incredibly Liverpool had wrapped up the title with seven games still to play.

There were still four matches remaining when Henderson's season came to a sudden halt. Ten minutes from time at Brighton's Amex Stadium Jordan sustained a knee injury that ruled him out for the remaining games. He had signed off with a spectacular goal, a first timer from outside the box which highlighted a typically forceful performance as Liverpool won yet again.

After a spell in a knee brace, two weeks later Jordan donned full kit as he received the Premier League trophy. Handing it over was the last Liverpool manager to win the league, the man who signed him; Sir Kenny Dalglish, the coronavirus requiring King Kenny to don a Liverpool logo'd face mask.

Following an exciting 5-3 win over a determined Chelsea, who had a Champions League place to play for, the trophy presentation was a spectacular affair. The fans could not be present inside the stadium but the spirit of the Kop was key to the affair as a specially constructed platform had been erected on the Kop for the trophy ceremony to take place.

As captain, Hendo came to the platform last to join his team mates, manager and staff who had already received their medals. Despite his knee injury Jordan didn't disappoint. The trademark trophy lift shuffle was there as he raised the biggest prize of all. After never having won the Premier League, for Liverpool to be champions was the coronation that for Reds more than matched even the triumph of the Champions League.

As fireworks and a light show Pink Floyd would be proud of engulfed Anfield, Hendo having had his moment of glory made sure everyone else had their own. Amidst the ecstatic celebrations the skipper could be seen pushing forward anyone who had yet to have a turn at their own trophy lift. It summed him up – always looking out for everyone.

"Walking up there was amazing" he admitted shortly afterwards. "The lads enjoyed the moment. The families were up there watching, which was a big thing for us. It's been an amazing season and to crown it off like that was really special...Winning the Premier League has always been a dream of mine since I was a kid. That's one of the reasons I came to Liverpool. You want to win trophies. The expectation is so high but when you come as a young player it is so difficult. It has been a process, it has been a journey. It just hasn't happened overnight."

It has taken almost a decade for some to realise why the likes of Steven Gerrard and Jurgen Klopp rate Jordan Henderson so highly and there are still some who don't see all he contributes but there is now a banner on the Kop with a picture of Hendo holding the Champions League trophy. "It is special" admits Jordan. "To be part of the club's history and to see that banner on the Kop, you never get used to it, to be honest! I just try to use it as even more motivation to make sure I do everything I can for this football club and this team to be successful, which I've always tried to do."

Jamie Carragher is another Liverpool legend firmly in the Jordan Henderson fan club. "I have to say I am delighted but a little bit baffled that Jordan Henderson is getting more praise this season than in previous years" he commented during the coronavirus lockdown. "I think that probably says more about those suggesting he has massively improved rather than the player himself because, as I'm sure Jurgen Klopp will testify, his consistent excellence as captain has been fundamental to Liverpool's return to the top."

Interviewed by Sky's Jeff Shreeves moments after lifting the Premier League trophy, Hendo was asked, "You are one of the most down to earth guys in football. How do you feel about the plaudits that have come your way this season, saying how you are the heir to Steven Gerrard's crown and how you have taken your game to the very next level?"

"It is obviously nice to hear good things" replied Jordan, allowing himself eight words of limelight before returning to his deeply held conviction. Swiftly he continued, "but it's not really about me. It's about the team. I wouldn't be where I'm at today without the players I've played with since I've been at Liverpool, the management that I've had, the coaches that I've worked with. These last few years have been immense and helped me massively. I'm lucky enough to be part of this football club, lucky enough to work with some amazing people who have helped me but I've always tried to give everything I've got. I've always tried to improve every single season and that won't stop."

Listening to Hendo deflect praise Jamie Carragher interjected, "You won't get it out of him but you'll get it out of me" he said, "He's had a monumental season. A legendary figure now in Liverpool's history."

That legendary status was further added to less than 48 hours later as Hendo was named as the Football Writers' Association men's Footballer of the Year. Such an accolade is a pinnacle in any player's career and many great names have hung up their boots without ever receiving the honour.

England boss Gareth Southgate was one of the first to congratulate Hendo. He said, "Jordan's the epitome of selfless commitment to the team and so it's extra special that he is being personally recognised for the way he's played, led the club and role modelled off the field to help wider society. I'm delighted for him and his family."

What about Jordan himself? Was this a time to allow himself a moment in the spotlight after being recognised for his superb achievement? To have done so would have been entirely out of character. Typically his response was one of a sharing nature that many would benefit from emulating.

Responding to the award Hendo had this to say, "I'd like to say how appreciative I am of the support of those who voted for me and the Football Writers' Association in general. You only have to look at the past winners of it, a number of whom I've been blessed to play with here at Liverpool, like Stevie [Gerrard], Luis [Suarez] and Mo [Salah] to know how prestigious it is. But as grateful as I am I don't feel like I can accept this on my own. I don't feel like anything I've achieved this season or in fact during my whole career has been done on my own. I owe a lot to so many different people – but none more so than my current teammates – who have just been incredible and deserve this every bit as much as I do. We've only achieved what we've achieved because every single member of our squad has been brilliant. And not just in matches. Not just in producing the moments that make the headlines and the back pages but every day in training. The players who've started the most games for us this season have been as good as they have been because of our culture and our environment at Melwood. No one individual is responsible for that – it's a collective effort and that's how I view accepting this honour. I accept it on behalf of this whole squad, because without them I'm not in a position to be receiving this honour. These lads have made me a better player – a better leader and a better person. If anything I hope those who voted for me did so partly to recognise the entire team's contribution. Individual awards are nice and they are special and I will cherish this one. But an individual award without the collective achievement wouldn't mean anywhere as much to me – if anything at all."

# CHAPTER THREE
# NEVER REPLACE STEVIE G

"The day they sacked me, they said you made a big mistake with Jordan Henderson." So revealed Liverpool's former director of football strategy Damien Comolli. Signing a 20-year old already capped by England before he came to Anfield was deemed a 'big mistake' by Liverpool's then owners according to Comolli, who was dismissed from his role in the year following Henderson's acquisition.

"I said, 'Are you sure?' and they said 'Yes, it's a big mistake'. I said I thought they were wrong, but what can I say? They are the owners of the club and if they want to make that decision then they make that decision. I was convinced he would be special. I was convinced he would be a Liverpool captain because he had all the attributes as a player and as a person. I'm delighted to see what he's achieved and I think there is a lot more to come."

Having been given a budget of £15m Comolli narrowly exceeded that although his initiative proved enormously costly to himself rather than the club. "It was very difficult for Kenny [manager Dalglish] and I to get £15 million from the owners for Jordan. Sunderland chairman Niall Quinn wanted a lot more than £15 million. He said I didn't realise how good he was, his character and personality. He said the last time they played a derby against Newcastle, towards the end of the game Jordan took a free-kick and the ball flew into the stands and he got a lot of stick from the Newcastle fans. He said the following week Jordan took 300 free-kicks in training because he was so mad with himself. I put the phone down and thought if that's the type of personality he is then we should do everything we possibly can to get him. I went up to £16.75 million to the great displeasure of the owners who absolutely slaughtered me on the phone."

Sacked at the end of Henderson's first season on Merseyside, manager Dalglish had himself cost Liverpool a British record £440,000 when signed from Celtic in 1977, the manager agreeing that fee being Hendo's fellow Wearsider Bob Paisley. Revealing the above story to The Athletic in February 2020 Comolli continued,

"I called Kenny and said: 'You need to help me on this one.' He said: 'It's a great deal, I'll tell them you did a great deal.'"

It wasn't just the Liverpool board and bean counters who felt that Henderson's signing was not a good one at the time despite the views of Dalglish and Comolli. There are high standards at Liverpool where only the best is good enough and anything approaching second rate is quickly ditched.

During that summer of 2011 when Liverpool lashed out for Henderson £23.5m was paid by Chelsea for 23-year old Valencia midfielder Juan Mata, while £33m took 22-year old Alexis Sanchez from Udinese to Barcelona with the European champions also investing £34m to bring in 24-year old Cesc Fabregas from Arsenal. Within the Premier League Manchester City spent a reported £24m on Arsenal's 24-year old Samir Nasri, a player in the final year of his contract. These were all players capable of playing the sort of silky, 'sexy' football Ruud Gullit once extolled.

Apparently lacking the flair or exotic attraction of these overseas stars, the signing of a lad from the north-east coast with few, if any, of the show-boating You-tube moments people often look for when there's a big new signing Henderson evidently under-whelmed many of Liverpool's world-wide followers. His You-tube highlights mainly being a very old Soccer AM skills drill and some tricks Jordan apparently uploaded himself as a young teenager in a kickabout in his street.

As the Reds' first signing of the summer of 2011 Hendo didn't excite. Arriving a week and a day before his 21st birthday the player himself however was thrilled and said all the right things, something he has consistently continued to do. Giving his first interview to the Liverpool website Jordan enthused, "I'm over the moon, overjoyed to be here and I'm really looking forward to it. Obviously it's hard to leave your local club. I'm a Sunderland lad, I've supported them all my life but I'm really looking forward to the future now and obviously this is a massive opportunity for me. I'm really excited by it.

Joining Jordan as new signings were fellow midfielder Charlie Adam from Blackpool, goalkeeper Doni from Roma, left-back Jose Enrique from Newcastle, Craig Bellamy, returning for a second spell from Manchester City, Uruguayan centre-back Sebastian Coates from Nacional and £20m wide-man Stewart Downing from Aston Villa.

Early signs failed to alter the immediate impression many had that Henderson might be a man for the future but he wasn't the man to slot straight into Liverpool's line-up. First featuring in a 3-0 friendly defeat at Hull he was then substituted after an hour of his competitive debut. That opening day match at Anfield pitted Henderson against his former club Sunderland who held the Reds to a 1-1 draw, one of the men signed to replace Henderson, free transfer Sweden international Seb Larsson, scoring a spectacular volley.

Not helping Henderson's cause in creating a positive impression with his new fans was that before any debates about not being able to replace Steven Gerrard began to surface, Jordan first of all had to cope with being asked to effectively replace Maxi Rodriguez and Dirk Kuyt, the latter a genuine Kop cult-hero.

While he has since developed into a midfielder often at his most effective in a central position, be that as a sitter or in a more advanced role, Henderson's willingness to put the team first has meant that over the years he has been utilised in a variety of roles at Anfield, a trait he shares with that other magnificent team man James Milner. Nonetheless something of a myth was created that Henderson was out of position as an orthodox right midfielder. Coming through the ranks at Sunderland much of Jordan's early football at youth and first team level was played on the right of midfield.

Never a speed merchant in the Adama Traore or Raheem Sterling mould, neither were terrific wingers such as David Beckham or Nick Summerbee. The most important asset for wingers is their ability to provide dangerous crosses and Henderson's talent for accurately whipping a ball in from the right hand side has been seriously under-estimated and under-used over the years.

Evidently Henderson's contribution to his team, be that for club or country, has been deemed to be stronger in a central role and with good reason, but to judge him inadequate in a wide position ignores the quality he brings to that berth's most vital aspect. Add to that, unlike many wingers Henderson will never be found wanting when it comes to tracking back to assist his defence.

Replacing Stevie G would be asking a huge amount of anyone let alone a lad just turned 21 and coming to live in a strange city for the first time, other than for a loan to Coventry as a teenager – something Gerrard never had to do until he was

35 – but Henderson did open the scoring in only his second home game as Bolton were beaten to take Liverpool to the top of the Premier League. It was a good goal too. Coming in from the right, Henderson had a first shot blocked but kept his composure as he latched onto the rebound and curled an exquisite effort into the top corner with his weaker left foot.

Goals though would be few and far between for Jordan. He wouldn't score again until the final home game of the season. That 4-1 home win over Chelsea four days after losing to the same side in the FA Cup final enabled Liverpool to reach a tally of 24 home goals in a season – equalling their lowest ever. Being goal-shy wasn't helped by the same game seeing Downing (Still without a Premier League goal) miss a penalty as Liverpool became the first top-flight outfit since the start of the Premier League to fail with five spot-kicks in a season.

Asked to sum up his first campaign at Anfield straight after the match Jordan reflected, "I've enjoyed it. I've learned a lot since I've been here so hopefully it'll give me a lot of confidence going into the next season, but overall I've been happy with it. To be honest I think we've played quite well throughout the season at times but just haven't got the results. We need to put the results right and just keep playing the way that we know we can because we've got some brilliant players here." It was a typically positive and assured interview from a young man who remained entirely polite and civil in the face of whatever criticism came his way.

Jordan's goal in that win over Chelsea had seen him start the move just outside his own box and steam forward where for once his hard running earned some personal reward as John Terry lost his balance to allow the youngster a clear run on goal. He still had plenty of work to do but calmly picked his spot, placing a low right-footed shot into the bottom corner. As the ball hit the back of the net even the TV summariser, ex-Arsenal forward Alan Smith couldn't help but reference the difficulties Hendo had endured, "Jordan Henderson, he's taken a lot of stick this season in his debut campaign at Anfield but that was a really smart finish for him."

Signing off his first year at Anfield with such a well taken goal did Henderson no harm but he was a long way from winning over many of his club's fans as I'd found out for myself when sitting amongst Liverpool supporters at the FA Cup final.

As a neutral at the game but willing Jordan on as someone I'd known since long before he'd made a senior debut I was struck by how negative many of those around me were with regard to his contribution, which as ever was industrious and always aiming to be positive.

Liverpool had had their short-comings that year but Henderson went into that FA Cup final having already pocketed a winner's medal from the League Cup final just over two months earlier. While he was substituted by Craig Bellamy in that penalty shoot-out victory over Cardiff, nonetheless when the final whistle sounded on Liverpool's campaign against another Welsh outfit, Swansea, the simple fact was that Jordan had made more appearances for Liverpool that season than any of his team-mates.

It's always easy to look good in a winning team. Liverpool had done well in the cups but by their standards had struggled in the league, eighth place being no-where near good enough as manager Dalglish would discover with his dismissal. Regardless of rumblings of disquiet the youthful Henderson simply remained focussed on doing his best for the team every time he pulled on the shirt, something he did in 48 of his side's 51 fixtures. Nonetheless even the respected Liverpool website LFChistory.net remarked that, "At times he seemed a little lost and not really sure what his role in the team was." No doubt this was an honest appraisal of how Henderson's form was judged at the time but in an age when players from overseas are routinely expected to need a year to acclimatise, the contribution of a 21-year old having made his first transfer away from home was one that might have been more appreciated in the light of the fact he'd managed to play more than any of Liverpool's established senior stars.

Something that probably helped Henderson achieve this was midfielder Lucas rupturing his anterior cruciate ligament in a League Cup tie with Chelsea in November. This ruled the popular Brazilian out for the rest of the season, reducing competition in midfield although at the point of Lucas' misfortune Henderson had played a game more than Lucas had managed.

The culmination of appearances alone failed to impress students who looked for quality over quantity. In its ratings of Dalglish's signings two thirds of the way through the season the Daily Telegraph waded in with the following: "Jordan

Henderson is the kind of signing lovers of statistical analysis have wet dreams about. His athleticism ensures he covers more miles than his team mates and his pass completion rate is exceptional. What the stats don't reveal is his runs never take him into dangerous areas and most of his distribution involves a six-yard pass back to his full-back or centre-half. Henderson looks like he should be a complete midfielder, but decisive, defence splitting passes, ferocious shots and crunching tackles have been notoriously absent. He has youth on his side, and playing in a more central position will help him, but there will need to be a serious elevation in standard next season."

Criticism of really top players sometimes motivates them rather than deflates them. For all the praise heaped on the real crème de la crème the moments they often remember themselves are the near misses and might have beens where they believe they could have done better. Obviously everyone is human and no-one likes criticism but while some might take exception to critics, particularly ones who haven't experienced top-level sport from beyond the press box or stands, others react to it with an 'I'll show you attitude."

Jordan Henderson is the perfect example of this. As Damien Comolli discovered from Niall Quinn when negotiating his transfer and was told about Hendo's professionalism in practising. Hearing and seeing the flak he was receiving from some quarters simply made the player even more disciplined. Like Kevin Keegan before him, Henderson has never been a player blessed with being born with the most natural talent but like Special K whatever talent he does have he has worked exceptionally hard to make the most of. In some respects this mentality is the greatest asset any footballer can have. Football is littered with wayward geniuses who never had to work on the talent they were born with but ultimately didn't make the most of their natural ability.

In Andy Carroll's case many of his problems have been down to bad luck with injuries but nonetheless the man who arrived at Anfield for almost double Henderson's price in the transfer window before Jordan's purchase - a British record £35m - has not reached the heights his ability in the air would suggest. At the time of writing Carroll is 31 and has fewer than 10 England caps and other than a Championship medal with Newcastle has just a League Cup winner's medal won with Liverpool to show for his career.

Reflecting on why the striker failed to become a great at Anfield, former teammate Craig Bellamy spoke to Sky Sports in 2018 and noted, "I don't believe he worked hard enough during the week to be the player he wanted to become. I never saw an inch of that, like with Jordan Henderson. He was going through a difficult period at that time as well, but he just trained and trained and trained, he kept improving, going to the gym. He worked, and I knew, I remember saying to him, 'You're going to be a top player. I know it, just by your attitude, and the ability you have, it will come'. I never felt that was going to be the case with Andy."

Like Carroll, Jamie Carragher was a team-mate on the day Jordan made his debut. Now a prominent Sky Sports summariser, Carragher – a player who like Henderson made the absolute most of his ability through force of personality and an inherent natural willingness to get stuck in – saw first-hand the driving force behind Hendo. "Jordan cost Liverpool £20million when he came from Sunderland in 2011, and Kenny Dalglish, the manager at the time, wanted to find a place for him in the team, and he initially played a lot of games on the right of midfield. It took him time to find his feet. He could be a very intense character back then who would get frustrated and emotional at times, but I remember him having a spat with Luis Suarez in training one day and I just thought, 'Do you know what? He has something.' "They didn't come to blows or anything like that, but Jordan and Luis clashed over something and exchanged words, but Jordan stood up to him. That's not easy as a young player, especially with Luis being one of the older, established pros, but it showed Jordan's determination, and a lot of us, myself included, wanted him to do well because he was so enthusiastic and clearly hungry to succeed."

"At the time I was trying to do the best I could do and it comes as a footballer, the criticism and people doubting you," Henderson later told Carragher on The Greatest Game podcast. "At the time I was a young player and there was one or two things Luis did in training that I didn't like and it made me feel like I wasn't good enough to be in the same team. The arms would go up – it was like, 'what's he doing', as if I shouldn't be there. It really hurt and frustrated me. He did it one, two, three times and then I exploded and I was ready to kill him! But from that point I had a really good relationship with Luis, I actually set him up the game after that."

In any workplace in the country, not just football teams, fellow workers know who are the grafters and who are the shirkers. Evidently seasoned pro's like Bellamy and Carragher could see Henderson's ambition was matched by his appetite to make things happen rather than wait for them to happen.

Capped six times by England at Under 21 level during his first season with Liverpool; and scoring against Azerbaijan at Watford, Jordan became England's Under 21 Player of the Year for 2012. His initial campaign at Anfield also saw him named as Liverpool's Young Player of the Year, the third year in a row he'd won such an award at club level following two at Sunderland.

All this contributed to former Liverpool manager Roy Hodgson calling Henderson up to the full England squad at the end of the season. In what was Hodgson's first match in charge of the national side Henderson came off the bench for the last 17 minutes of a 1-0 friendly win over Norway in Oslo, a sub for Gareth Barry who had himself replaced Gerrard at half time. Perhaps it was true, Henderson would never replace Stevie G, Barry had done that.

Having previously played for England at Wembley, the match at the Ulleval Stadium was Henderson's away debut at full international level. He only had a week to wait for his first Wembley appearance for England as a Liverpool player, this time getting the last seven minutes as again England held on to a slender 1-0 advantage, this time against Belgium. Hendo's discipline and energy evidently being valued by England's vastly experienced manager who trusted him to help the national side see the game out – not least as this time the man Jordan was replacing was none other than Stevie G after all.

With Frank Lampard injured Henderson made the cut for the Euro 2012 finals. With the score tied at 1-1 in the opening game against France in Ukraine Jordan replaced Scott Parker to face the same side he had encountered on his debut before coming to Liverpool. Following England's opening draw Jordan was left on the bench as Hodgson's side negotiated narrow wins over Sweden and the host nation to progress to the quarter-finals.

Again Henderson watched the 90 minutes from the side-lines, itching to get on and his chance came four minutes into extra-time when again Parker was the man to give way as Jordan joined club-mates Gerrard, Glen Johnson and Andy Carroll.

The game in Kiev finished goalless before England went out on penalties, Gerrard and Wayne Rooney scoring but the Ashleys of Young and Cole failing to beat Gianluigi Buffon after Andrea Pirlo's Panenka penalty had turned the tide at a time when England held the advantage.

England were out but as the second youngest member of England's side – Henderson's big mate Danny Welbeck who he had played with at Sunderland being the youngest – Jordan ended his first season at Liverpool with plenty of evidence of success. He had been capped four times at the end of the season, played in a European quarter-final, won the League Cup, played in the FA Cup final, won Liverpool's Young Player of the Year and England Under 21 Player of the Year awards and made more appearances for Liverpool than any other player. Hardly a disaster for a 21-year old trying to make his way in the game in the face of negativity.

For Henderson though it was never about winning personal accolades, it was about improvement and then improving again. For top characters like Jordan it is not about reaching a destination but seeing how far and how purposefully the journey can take you.

Steven Gerrard was already a legendary player and one who absolutely deserves that status. Henderson himself was more interested in learning from the best, not replacing him. As Jordan said when he came to Merseyside, "Steven Gerrard is one of the best players in the world, you want to be playing with him and training with him to try and improve yourself as a player."

Stevie G himself had nothing to fear from anyone. His place in Liverpool folklore was long since assured but like anyone who understands how teams succeed rather than individuals he came to appreciate exactly what Jordan Henderson brings to a successful side. Writing in his newspaper column in the week Jordan captained Liverpool to Champions League glory in 2019 Gerrard said, "If I had to name someone I regard as the ultimate professional, then Jordan would come right at the top of the list. He is selfless, he puts himself at the back of the queue because he looks after everyone else first. He puts Jordan Henderson last."

More recently in April 2020 as Hendo's Reds closed in on Premier League triumph Rangers boss Gerrard warmed to his theme, telling BT Sport Jordan is a "Very fit, athletic boy who is very selfless in how he approaches his play on the pitch. He puts everyone else before himself and when you play alongside him you appreciate the job he does for the team. I think over the years he has developed parts of his game, his passing range is fantastic and he's running games with control a bit like Paul Scholes used to do it. He's leading by example and he is always there for the team. I've watched him grow with interest as a person. He's always been a great lad, a great teammate, unbelievable human being and it's no surprise that people are now starting to recognise what a man he is, on and off the pitch. Every bit of praise he gets as a player and as a human being he deserves it because it's true. I can guarantee it because I've experienced it alongside him."

For all their superstars Brazil have never replaced Pele. England have never replaced Bobby Moore and Liverpool may well never replace Stevie G. However Hendo has emulated Gerrard in lifting the Champions League and surpassed him in leading Liverpool to the Premier League title. As an individual player he may well not be as good as Gerrard but in a team game his ability to get the best out of his team as well as himself should not be underestimated. Ultimately whether Hendo is as good as Gerrard in immaterial. What matters is they are both great players and inspirational captains. Each of them hold the other in the highest esteem and surely they are the best qualified people to know what matters. Born almost exactly ten years apart, Jordan came along at just the right time to learn from Stevie and go on to carry the torch.

## CHAPTER FOUR

# CHOOSING TO BE DIFFERENT

The selflessness of Hendo's that Steven Gerrard spoke about was something Jordan grew up with. He came into the Sunderland Academy shortly after the first Harry Potter book was published in the month Jordan turned seven. Harry Potter's rise to fame was a damn sight quicker than Jordan's as the work that goes into developing a top footballer takes many years and involves the help of a lot of people along the way.

Jordan had first appeared in the Sunderland programme before his first birthday! As Sunderland battled to stay up, a photo of him in a red and white striped top, captioned 'Young supporter Jordan Henderson, born on 17th June 1990' appeared in the match programme for a 0-0 draw with Arsenal. It was a game that provided the Gunners with the point that secured the 1991 league title when Liverpool subsequently lost at Forest two days later as Arsenal overcame Manchester United.

Joining the Sunderland Academy was not quite the first step on the ladder to success. As a six and seven year old Jordan had sported an Inter Milan like kit playing for Fulwell Juniors. At this age he was coached by Ian Dipper who remembers, "Even then you could see he had a passion to play. I think his mam had a big influence on that. She's always run her own aerobics classes and you could always tell that she knew what she wanted to do and was very driven in the way that Jordan is. I first coached Jordan when I was working with Mitch Whellans who had a company called Mr. Football. We used to train at Fulwell Junior School and he used to come along. We used to do two hours training with him each week. He was a quiet lad but you could see he was already really dedicated. He was full of skills and loved a trick. He was always a good listener and took everything on board."

Having started at the Sunderland Academy Hendo progressed in a cohort that included striker Martyn Waghorn, whose career has included excelling at Rangers and Derby County, and midfielder Jack Colback, who after over 100 games for Sunderland and recognition at England Under 20 level was called into a full

England squad after his move to Newcastle only to have to withdraw through injury.

As Jordan got older his coaches included the former Wimbledon midfielder Carlton Fairweather – twice a Wombles scorer against Liverpool – and Steve Golightly, a former Sunderland youth teamer who had a massive influence on Jordan as he was also his PE teacher at Farringdon Community Academy. There Jordan was friends with Scott Borthwick who was in his year group and went on to play international cricket for England.

In his early years at Sunderland Jordan came under the influence of Lewis Dickman. "I had Lewis at a very early age" Hendo recalled when talking about his early development at the club when he returned to play at the Stadium of Light for England in 2016. "He was all about enjoyment, bringing confidence into younger lads. That's so important at that age. Sometimes people can get too serious and by the time they get to 15 or 16 they start falling out of love with the game. But I was fortunate to have Lewis coach me. He's a brilliant character who I still speak to now."

Hendo also came under the guidance of academy manager Ged McNamee and coach Elliott Dickman, brother of Lewis and a former England youth player who was assistant academy manager during the time Hendo was coming through the ranks. "As I got older Elliott was a big part of my career" Jordan continued, "...Elliott really pushed to keep me on." Fairweather and Dickman were strong advocates for Jordan being awarded a Scholarship as school leaving age arrived. As with all players, at this point coaching staff come together to discuss the strengths and weaknesses of each player, be those pros and cons to do with ability, attitude or whatever else.

Speaking to Rio Ferdinand for his Locker Room series in June 2020 Jordan looked back at that time, "There was a period when I was around 16 when you left school and you got a scholarship or you didn't. That was a key period because I think I was touch and go at that time because I had a big growing spurt and my body was a bit all over the place and my coordination wasn't there. But the coaches saw my work ethic and I had the quality as well and fortunately enough I made sure I took it and learned and tried to be the best player I could possibly be."

As Jordan was about to step up to the Under 18 side Kevin Ball was assistant academy manager. Considering the discussion concerning whether to offer Hendo a scholarship he says, "If I remember rightly what was discussed at the time is us talking about players coming in and the question that got asked was about Jordan's physicality. He was slight in comparison to the others." At the time Jordan was 182cm / 5'9" and 67kg / 10 stone five pounds. Kevin continues, "I remember speaking to Elliott and we spoke about his attitude and ability and would the physicality be a problem. To be fair to Elliott Dickman he raved about Jordan in terms of his attitude and ability, and so did Carlton, so I just said 'It's a no-brainer for me.' Let's face it if we hadn't offered him a contract he would have become the player that got away without question."

Ball twice captained Sunderland to promotion, including the record breaking 105 point season of 1998-99 under Peter Reid when Henderson was a young kid in the Academy. Ball also went on to serve the club as caretaker manager. He is a massive personality on Wearside, looked upon quite rightly as one of the club's best ever captains and remains a club ambassador. Originally a centre back who became a midfielder after playing against Liverpool in the 1992 FA Cup final, Bally invariably gave absolutely everything he had on the pitch and demanded the same from everyone else. As with Henderson now the team level could drop a notch if he wasn't there to lead both by example and vocality.

Hendo had the perfect person as coach in Ball. Kevin is renowned for his exceptional professionalism. "I think Bally had a massive influence on him as a 16 to 19 year old" says Ian Dipper who after coaching the six and seven year old Jordan went on to also coach at the club's academy. Jordan himself says, "Kevin Ball was brilliant in terms of character and knowledge of football. Discipline was so important. Changing rooms, boots, facilities, everything had to be spot on before you could leave the building. It was very strict but I loved every minute of it and it really put us in good stead. I still use those morals today in the way that I think and do things, not just in football but in the way I lead my life."

Put it to Bally that this is his influence rubbing off on Jordan and he will have none of it. "I saw that in him years and years ago when he came into the academy. I saw in Jordan what I was more like later in my career. I didn't see in him what I was first like because I wasn't dedicated like he was when I was young.

When I first went to Coventry I had it all wrong attitude wise. When I look back my beginnings were the opposite of Jordan's beginnings. Everything I did wrong at Coventry Jordan did right at Sunderland. I learned from what went wrong for me at Coventry but it was incredible for me to watch Jordan and some of the other lads at Sunderland be so positive and so professional when they first came in. They were demanding of me in terms of what we did. They were so inquisitive and demanding of themselves because they all had aspirations of themselves to want to be footballers and that in itself is something that I think is a fantastic tool to have."

Scott Pearce was the Academy Sports Scientist at the time and concurs. "Jordan was in my first group when I first came into the club. [Fitness coach] Scott Ainsley made me aware of his physical status. Jordan was a late physical maturer and we had to be aware of that around training. He might have been late developing physically but mentally I always thought he was streets ahead of everyone. It was just getting the balance right in terms of challenging him mentally and also making sure we didn't hamper him from a physical point of view. He was a sponge. He'd ask questions of me and the physios and he took everything in. He was ruthless and single minded."

That sponge-like ability to take in as much information as possible extended far and wide. Under the club's Education and Welfare manager, the late Brian Buddle, like the rest of his group Jordan spent some of his scholarship time in the classroom doing an apprenticeship in Sporting Excellence (ASE). "It is work based learning and covers a number of topics" Jordan explained to me at the time. "There are times in our week when we are devoted to this and a number of different people work with us. Some of the main areas are Technical and Tactical Development, Mental Fitness and Health and Safety. The Apprenticeship is over two years. There is an academic element and we take the level two coaching award. It is a good course which motivates you because you get a certificate or two at the end of it plus you find out what your weaknesses are and work on them."

It was an important part of the 'Plan B' Sunderland and other clubs concerned about the future of their young players carry out. One of Jordan's team mates who did not progress to top grade football was Richard Smith who went on to study at Harvard and Oxford, the academic equivalent of winning the Champions League.

"The overriding thing was you always knew that in every game he played you would always get out of Jordan Henderson whatever he had to give at that time" explains Kevin Ball. "That could have been an unbelievably world class performance, a workmanlike performance or, if I'm honest, it might not have been a great performance but if that was the case it wouldn't have been for the want of trying. There was never ever a game where he didn't have a go. That was his mantra. People talk about giving more than 100% but I'm not a believer in that. I want people to give 100% and Jordan gave 100% all of the time and that is what he still does."

"Me and Bally used to talk about him all the time" continues Pearce. "The word sacrifice used to come up and I remember once over a coffee saying 'I don't like that word sacrifice. He didn't sacrifice anything. He just chose to be different. That's what struck me. He chose to be different. Kids of that age are impressionable. When they socialise alcohol might be involved but he would choose to go out with the lads and not drink. I'd be in the dressing room and the gym. The boys talk about these things and it often came up in conversation that Jordan had taken the car to wherever they were going but he wouldn't drink."

Henderson's debut at Under 18 level came on 8 April 2006 for a side at that point run by Elliott Dickman. He was 15 and starting against Manchester United on a day the Red Devils gave a debut to Danny Welbeck. Also debuting for the United side that day were Oliver Norwood and Scott Moffat as well as substitutes Joe Dudgeon, Cameron Stewart and Nick Ajose. The visitors also included Tom Cleverley, Craig Cathcart, Ben Amos, James Chester and Febian Brandy. Seven years later Henderson and Cleverley would come on together for England in a joint substitution in the FA's 150th year celebration match against Chile at Wembley. It was a long way from Sunderland's Academy of Light where Henderson was joined as a debutant by Josh Home-Jackson and David Hooper.

Later the same afternoon the first team's Barclays Premiership match with Fulham became the only Premier League game ever to be abandoned due to bad weather – as snow hit Wearside in April. The bad weather arrived mid-way through the second half of the Under 18 game which had kicked off at midday. Before the storm arrived Sunderland Under 18s had taken an early lead through Martyn Waghorn before Dubliner Chris Fagan equalised with a brilliant goal that was a replica of Frank Worthington's ITV Goal of the Season for Bolton against Ipswich in 1979.

Jordan's side then took control with a quick-fire double from England under 18 striker David Dowson before United pulled one back through Nicky Ajose as Sunderland won 3-2.

The following week Henderson was part of the youth squad that headed off to France for the Reze Tournament near Nantes. There he played in defeats to tournament winners Rennes as well as Sparta Prague and Anderlecht before helping Sunderland to a 1-0 win over the Madagascar national team, and finally a 0-0 draw against Niort who were then lost to on penalties.

On his return from France Hendo got a second league game in a 1-0 win at Sheffield Wednesday before his third and last Under 18 appearance of the season came in a 1-1 draw at home to newly crowned FA Youth Cup winners Liverpool. Kevin Ball's son Luke scored for the home side while Hendo went close to a winner, Liverpool keeper Paul Lancaster finger-tipping away Jordan's shot before substitute Jonathan Pringle equalised with a penalty.

Under Kevin Ball Jordan was part of an Under 18 side that won their league for the next two seasons as well as reaching the final of the FA Premier Academy Play-offs and the semi-final of the FA Youth Cup.

During 2006-07 as Roy Keane's first team won the Championship, Jordan started by gaining the experience of playing against the youth teams of Hertha Berlin, Helsingborg of Sweden and Cruzeiro of Brazil as well as domestic opposition in pre-season. He then went on to play virtually every game as Sunderland Under 18s won their league to qualify for the play-offs. Those play-offs saw Hendo help Sunderland to beat Manchester City 3-2 at the Stadium of Light before he scored directly from a corner in the final against Leicester before a crowd of over four and a half thousand at the same ground. His side would finish as runners up after a 2-2 draw as they lost 4-3 on penalties, Hendo not being one of the takers having been substituted by Jordan Cook.

Having been subject of a takeover by Niall Quinn's Drumaville consortium the previous summer Sunderland had not entered a reserve team into a league during Hendo's first season as an Academy regular. Under former Everton midfielder Kevin Richardson, instead they played regular friendlies, Hendo getting his first game at that level a week before Christmas in 2006, playing in a young side that beat York City 1-0 at Sunderland's training base the Academy of Light. The following month he got his second and final reserve team outing of 2006-07 when part of a much more experienced team that beat Hibs 1-0 at the Stadium of Light. Former Liverpool full back Stephen Wright, Martin Fulop, Clive Clarke, Tommy Miller, Andy Welsh and Kenny Cunningham were amongst the senior players he played alongside for the first time that day.

2007-08 saw Jordan increasingly involved with the reserves, who had joined the Barclays Premier Reserve League North, as well as remaining a regular as the Under 18s retained their league title. During the course of the campaign former Manchester United youth coach Neil Bailey took over the reserve team who won the Durham Challenge Cup.

Over the course of the season the 17-year old made 13 league and cup appearances for the second team and while he didn't score he did net twice in a reserve team friendly with Bradford City in January.

In his senior career Jordan has taken criticism for not scoring enough goals with little regard being given to his role in the team. He does have goals in him however. As Sunderland Under 18s won their league he hit ten goals from a wide right position in league and cup (from 27+4 games), finishing third top scorer behind Martyn Waghorn and Nathan Luscombe.

Waghorn has gone on to have a long career at a good level, mainly in the Championship while Luscombe made just one competitive first team appearance for Sunderland. A talented and exciting player Luscombe had the ability to have made more of his professional career but had various off field issues which were ultimately too difficult to overcome. Even as a teenager Henderson recognised this and did his level best to take fellow winger Luscombe under his wing. "Talk about endearing qualities as a captain. Jordan Henderson looked after Nathan Luscombe like he was his brother" remembers Ball of Hendo's help to a player Pearce describes as, "Without doubt the most talented player I've ever seen at youth team level" adding "I remember one game against Sheffield United and I'm pretty sure they had four right backs by the end of the game. He terrorised them."

Nathan Luscombe joins the ranks of talents lost to football. Like Hendo he might have gone on to play for Liverpool rather than Hartlepool which is where he ended up after one FA Cup appearance for Sunderland, drifting out of league football after just 26 league games, all but five of them as substitute.

While sadly Nathan Luscombe's potential was never fully realised, Henderson went on to maximise his own ability. Jordan's leadership qualities were recognised as he started to stand in for Jack Colback as captain. The second time he did this was at Liverpool in October 2007, four days after first sporting the armband against Huddersfield.

Progress was rapid for Hendo at this point. The following month he got his first taste of being involved with the first team. Former Celtic man Keane took Sunderland to Falkirk during an international break to play a Testimonial for Andy Lawrie, a defender who had already left Falkirk after 11 years' service to join St. Johnstone. On a night that Andy Cole played for Sunderland Jordan was given the last half an hour of a 1-1 draw. "It was a great experience" enthused Hendo afterwards Waggy [Martyn Waghorn] and Conor came on as well and I thought all three of us did well on the night. The game gave us all a little taste of what it's like to be involved with the first team."

Joining Henderson and Colback in Sunderland's midfield by now was Conor Hourihane who has subsequently gone on to star for Aston Villa and the Republic of Ireland, although he didn't get a break in the north-east. "Conor Hourihane would be open and honest and say that Jordan had a massive impact on him" says Scott Pearce. "Conor came in as a first year when Jordan was a second year. Conor looked at Jordan Henderson and took it as the norm. This is how I should behave as a youth team player and there were probably another three or four players on the back of that who did the same."

The month after the taster for the youngsters at Falkirk Waghorn became the first of Henderson's year group to get a competitive first team debut, becoming at that point Sunderland's youngest Premier League player when he lined up against Manchester United. As always, seeing one of their colleagues break through provided great encouragement to the rest of the Under 18s with Jordan disclosing, "My aims are to play regular reserve team football but also to break into the first team. I've seen it can be done now with Martyn getting in there. I've had a little taste of it myself in the testimonial at Falkirk and hopefully it'll come for me."

With twelve players in their squad who went on to play league football clearly Jordan was part of a cracking young team. Their run to the semi-finals of the FA Youth Cup in 2008 brought the best out of them.

Henderson got the run started before Christmas when he opened the scoring from fully 40 yards at the Stadium of Light as he latched onto a poor clearance from Norwich goalkeeper Luke Emson. On a night where Jordan shone with a sublime range of passing and Waghorn helped himself to a hat-trick the Canaries were beaten 6-1, as Sunderland scored six in the competition for the first time since the second leg of the 1969 final.

A Macclesfield side featuring Wayne Rooney's brother John proved to be sterner opposition in the next round as Sunderland progressed 2-1 to set up another home tie, this time with Liverpool. Holders for the previous two seasons Liverpool took part in an outstanding exhibition of attacking football as Sunderland eventually won 5-3 after extra time.

A couple of weeks before that Youth Cup thriller with Liverpool Jordan had been part of the first team squad for a Premier League game at Anfield. He and Jack Colback were included in the travelling party of 18. Back then there were five subs rather than seven so neither got on the bench but it was a taster for them of being involved with the big boys and for Jordan prescient that it should be for a game at Liverpool. Having seen Stevie G wrap up a 3-0 win from the penalty spot at the time Hendo's thoughts were about getting into Sunderland's team let alone succeeding Gerrard at Anfield, but the journey had started.

A week later it took another step forward when along with Waghorn, Cook and Luscombe he was given a professional contract with Academy manager Ged McNamee noting, "All of these lads deserve their contracts... They have earned contracts because of the potential they have shown and to have three of this year's U18 in the first team squad of 18 for a game away to Liverpool is very pleasing. [Waghorn had played] Some of these lads have been with us for a long time. It does take time to bring players through because it isn't a quick fix to produce players."

The quarter-final of the FA Youth Cup took Sunderland to the Valley to face Charlton. The Addicks main man was Jonjo Shelvey. It was his 16th birthday and he took every free-kick, every corner and just about every throw in it seemed.

Everything went through Shelvey who was outstanding and had Scott Wagstaff alongside him. Wagstaff has gone on to have a long career in the game at a lower level, most famously scoring twice as AFC Wimbledon knocked West Ham out of the FA Cup in 2019.

Despite Shelvey's outstanding display Sunderland were the better team and won the game 2-1. The match looked like going into extra time when a minute into injury time with the game locked at 1-1 Hendo spotted keeper Joe Wolley off his line and coolly lobbed the ball home from the edge of the box to delight the 500 visiting fans in the crowd of 1800. It wasn't just the fans who were delighted, Kevin Ball admits, "The funny thing was when Jordan scored it was the first time I'd ever run down the touchline with happiness. It was just a pivotal moment and it was such a class goal from Jordan."

Hendo himself went off in a sprint of exuberant joy in celebration but afterwards, despite having made a goal for Waghorn with a pin-point floated cross in addition to his dramatic winner, was still heaping praise on others. "I'm very pleased with scoring and making goals but it's about the team rather than individuals" he told me, adding, "In any game the people who score or set goals up tend to get the headlines but it is the team who win games and I thought the back four were outstanding." The quote illustrates how Hendo has never changed. At the time he was still 17 but he already understood that the team comes first. It remains the mantra he preaches now in his thirties as one of the most decorated players in the game.

The late winner at The Valley was Hendo's third in as many games having scored in recent league wins over Derby and Huddersfield. The strike at Huddersfield was, "One of the best solo goals I've ever seen" according to Kevin Ball. Jordan himself as usual was playing down his individual contribution, explaining, "I was on the edge of the box and 'megged' two players in a row and stuck it in the bottom corner. I'm obviously pleased with any goal but it is always about the team. No team wins a game because of what one player does it's about what the team as a whole does."

There would be another cracker to come in the youth cup semi-final against Manchester City where he came up against future Liverpool teammate Daniel

Sturridge on a night when for the first time Hendo's face beamed down from the match programme cover.

Three years later future Northern Ireland international Ryan McGivern would make his only Premier League appearance for Manchester City against Sunderland. The full back scored both goals from corners in the first leg of the semi on Wearside as City won 2-0 but in the second leg at the City of Manchester stadium Hendo halved City's advantage with a 20 yarder after only quarter of an hour. From then on he dominated the game as his side looked to retrieve the deficit. In the 87th minute they were convinced they had done so as Ryan Noble netted only for a hotly disputed offside flag to cut short the celebrations after the referee initially gave the goal, Henderson being one of three players cautioned for their protests.

Having surprised City by switching from their usual 4-4-2 to 4-3-3 with Henderson tucked in, Jordan had gone closest to squaring the tie on aggregate with a brilliant piece of play where he lifted the ball over two defenders before smashing the dropping ball inches over the bar from the angle of the penalty area. It was a touch of class that added to the increasingly favourable impression Jordan was making on the watching Roy Keane.

Disappointment with not going on to the FA Youth Cup final was compensated for as the team strode on to retain their league title. A 6-1 win at runners' up Nottingham Forest meant the league had been won by a double digit distance with 24 goals scored in the last five games, Henderson scoring in a 5-1 win at Manchester United. Simultaneously he was also pushing on into the reserves, being part of another big win when Blackburn were battered 7-2.

Having won the league Sunderland were again paired with Manchester City in the Academy League Play Off Northern Final. Staged at SportCity rather than the Etihad this time City deservedly came out on top although an injury time Kieran Trippier penalty somewhat disguised how close City's 4-2 win had been. There was though another winners' medal to end the season with as Jordan helped the reserves to victory over Gateshead in the final of the Durham Challenge Cup, a grand trophy played for since the 1880s.

By now Hendo had shown himself to be a talent people needed to keep an eye on. Certainly people within the club knew he had the ability and attitude to mark him out as a future first teamer. Signing a new contract on 4 June, just under a fortnight before his 18th birthday Jordan was joined in the reserves by David Meyler. Signed by Keane from York City. Meyler went on to play for the Republic of Ireland and quickly found out how dedicated his new teammate was, "We might have to report for training at nine o'clock. He's in at eight, doing work in the gym. After training he's doing work outside, working on his passing. All that kind of stuff, he did it. I remember when we were 18 or 19 we would play a reserve game before we broke into the first team. If we won the whole team would go out but Jordan wouldn't. Jordan's never drank. He always had that desire, dedication, commitment to be successful."

Meyler came on for Sunderland Reserves in a pre-season friendly at Unibond League Premier side Kendal Town on a day when the players were presented to England immortal Tom Finney. Meyler came on with Sunderland leading 7-4 after trailing 1-4. Never satisfied, Henderson added two more goals including one a minute from time to make it 9-4.

That fight-back may well have been inspired by the aftermath of the reserves previous match. Eleven days earlier Jordan had been part of a team that had featured four full internationals as Conference North newcomers Gateshead reversed the previous season's cup final defeat by beating Sunderland's second string 2-0. Clearly the players didn't fancy returning to base after a potential loss to Kendal. Memories were still fresh of Roy Keane's reaction after Gateshead defeat and they have never been forgotten as Jordan revealed to Rio Ferdinand in June 2020, "I was in the reserves playing away at Gateshead. We had a pretty decent team out in the reserves and we ended up getting beat 2-0. I don't think Roy went to the game but his coaching staff did, and they rang him and told him what happened. On the coach back we got the shout that we needed to go back to the academy as the gaffer wanted to speak to us. As you can imagine, we've just been beat 2-0 and we've got the gaffer Roy Keane waiting for us to get there. I can remember it like it was yesterday. Being in the room in like a half-circle and he was basically just going through every player. I think he might have watched some of the game back on the video and he went through everyone and I was sweating, I was only a young lad. Sweating front and back thinking 'please don't come to me'.

But I remember it well because he did come to me and he sort of just asked us if

I thought I was good enough to play in the first team, which I answered yes, instinctively, even though I was sweating and nervous. I think he quite liked that. I didn't have the best of games to be honest, but you could see from the way I reacted that I was still trying to run about and trying to get back in the game. A few days later he called us into the first team and I made my debut against Ajax so he gave me my opportunity and I probably wouldn't be where I am today without that really."

In fact it was the day after the Gateshead debacle that Roy Keane gave Jordan the chance to see if he could cut it at first team level. Sunderland entertained Ajax with Henderson sent on to replace Teemu Tainio for the final 14 minutes. For five minutes he was on the pitch at the same time as Luis Suarez until the Urugayan was brought off on a day the Dutch side won with a goal from Klass Jan Huntelaar before Henderson entered the fray.

The friendly was the fifth of six pre-season games and the only one Henderson was involved in but as the season kicked off with a Premier League match at home to Liverpool Henderson had a first team squad number for the first time: number 42 with Meyler 41 and Hourihane 43.

Jordan wasn't involved in that game which Liverpool won 1-0 with a Fernando Torres goal seven minutes from time but he was edging ever closer to pushing himself into Roy Keane's team. His own season started with a reserve team derby against Newcastle United at St. James' Park. Almost nine years to the day since a famous 2-1 Sunderland win at the same venue led to Ruud Gullit's dismissal the score-line was repeated. Sweden international Rade Prica opened the scoring against United keeper Fraser Forster but as the following Sunderland match programme noted, "the credit was all Jordan Henderson's, the youngster's approach play tying the home defence in knots." After appearing in a cup win against Hartlepool, next time out in the league Hendo helped to another 2-1 win over Liverpool, this time at Bob Paisley Park.

Ten days later number 42 Henderson featured on a Premier League team-sheet for the first time. Jordan didn't get a game but was amongst the subs for a 2-1 defeat at Aston Villa where Djibril Cisse got Sunderland's goal. Jordan wasn't called upon in Sunderland's next four games but after a disappointing defeat at Stoke in the last of those Keane again put the eager youngster on the bench for a trip to Chelsea.

With Hendo watching from the sub's bench Chelsea ripped Sunderland apart. Keane's men held out until the 27th minute when Alex scored the Blues 1000th league goal and by half time it was 3-0. Steed Malbranque was a talented footballer but not the man to look to when being given a chasing. When Sunderland emerged from the dressing room in West London on that first day of November in 2008 Malbranque remained behind, Henderson having been put on in his place for a first team debut.

It was a baptism of fire. In Jordan's first eight minutes on the pitch he saw his team concede twice more, Frank Lampard registering his 100th league goal and Nicolas Anelka completing his hat-trick as Chelsea eased above Liverpool at the pinnacle of the Barclays Premier League. Nonetheless there was no further scoring as Henderson harried, chased and did all he could to prevent things getting any worse.

Jordan had done enough to be named on the bench again for the next three Premier League games without getting on but during this run he did get a start in a home Carling Cup defeat to Blackburn Rovers, Hendo getting 80 minutes under his belt. Three games later Keane parted company with Sunderland after a disagreement with Ellis Short, an American who had invested heavily in the team and would soon become outright owner.

Coach Ricky Sbragia took over, gave Hendo a seat on the bench without using him at Everton at the end of December and then sent the teenager out on loan to Coventry where Jordan was to gain invaluable experience before picking up an injury.

By the time the next (2009-10) season arrived Steve Bruce would be in charge at Sunderland and Jordan would quickly become a regular member of the first team scene. His days as a member of the academy were over. Jamie Carragher and others from Anfield have spoken about a later incident where a still young Henderson refused to buckle as Luis Suarez showed his displeasure on the training ground. Scott Pearce recalls a similar incident at Sunderland. "I remember the first day he trained with Steve Bruce. It was a typical pre-season session and the boys were running. That might not be the case these days but they were then. That summer Jordan had been down at Silksworth running track with myself and Scott Ainsley along with a couple of other boys, Jamie Chandler and Jordan Cook. He had come back absolutely flying and he was way out in front. I think it was Anton Ferdinand gave it the old 'get back here you little so and so. Stop trying to embarrass us' I was just out watching and he turned round and told him where to go. I thought it was brilliant."

Jordan was not involved in first team training to make the numbers up. He had earned the right to be there, just as he had at Melwood when Suarez wasn't happy with him. Hendo was far from the finished article when he went to Liverpool and still wouldn't think he is now as he always looks to do better, but Kevin Ball describes how he developed at Sunderland.

"He played right wing. That was his position when he was younger. We played him in the centre in a three as well and sometimes in a two but he was excellent on the right wing. He had an ability to cross the ball that was fantastic. He never needed to beat his man. He'd just take a touch and whip it round hm. If that was blocked off he'd chop it back and stand it up with his left foot. I can remember a skill that he performed in the national play off final against Leicester, "In that play-off game the ball came to him in towards our defensive middle third. As it came to him the ball back got really tight so he was now facing his own goal. So he's run towards it and he's chopped the ball so it went half a yard forward and as the defender came forward as the ball hit the ground it span the other way so he still had it. I remember being stunned and thinking, 'how can you coach that?'

"I was honest with Jordan. It wasn't that I didn't think I couldn't coach Jordan but I was mindful that Jordan saw things quicker than I did. I had to be mindful of enabling his talent to flourish. I used to say to him ' In the defensive third Jordan, keep the ball. Middle third I said you can use your judgement as to whether to keep it or do something different if it's on but in the final third just play what you see.

"A lot of it is decision making and Jordan is excellent at that. I don't think Jordan has proved his doubters wrong. I think he's proved his backers right. I still read little bits and pieces of people still condemning him but to me Jordan epitomises a player who makes the most of what he's got. He maximises his ability and is everything you would want in a successful footballer. Every England manager has picked him because they trust him. You always knew you could trust Jordan.

You knew that however he played he would not be the one who ducked away or shied away but he would give it everything he had. It's a cliché to say something like that but it's fact. He's earned that respect by sheer enthusiasm

"When Jordan was 17 I told Scott Pearce he'd play for England but I told Scott to keep that between us. The day Jordan made his debut for England Scott told Jordan that and Jordan sent me a message after telling Scott he knew I always had faith in him." Ball hadn't had long to wait for his prediction to come true, Jordan became a full international when he was just 20.

Ball's admiration for Henderson is far from a one way street. In late February 2020 shortly before the lockdown Ball was honoured with a special award – the John Fotheringham award – at the North East Football Writers' Dinner at the Ramside Hall Hotel in Durham at which a message from Jordan acknowledged, "On a personal level, thank you for everything you've done for me. I don't think I would have achieved what I have without going through the experience I did with you at such a young age and the foundation that you set for me. Giving me responsibility at such a young age, I feel like I've taken all of that into my work today and I'll continue to do that. A massive thank you and a massive congratulations."

Ball's influence on Henderson continues to this day. The former Sunderland skipper keeps in touch with dozens of his former players not just superstars like the Jordans of Henderson and Pickford. Kevin keeps in contact with lads playing throughout the EFL and in non-league. They all know they can turn to him for advice if it is ever needed. In an age when so many people are belatedly thinking about the mental well-being of young men in the public eye Bally has always been an experienced pro they can always ask for advice. Glitz and glamour washes off Bally like water off a duck's back. What impresses Kevin is what impresses Jordan, honesty and integrity.

"My thoughts on him have never changed since he left the club" says Ball. "My parting statement to him was, 'Jordan if you become a big-time Charlie I'll come down there and kick you right up the backside'. I remember going down to Liverpool to meet him once. He was the captain of Liverpool and he had captained England and I watched him walk down the road when we were going to do an interview in a restaurant. He had on a hoodie and a pair of jeans. He was just a normal person. He could have been anybody. My thoughts on Jordan have never deviated. I've always known what his quality is and what his attitude is.

"It pleases me and simultaneously displeases me that people now see that because it was short-sighted not to see it in the beginning. After Kenny Dalglish signed him there was a time when Jordan was struggling down there. I always thought if I got the job at Sunderland he'd be the first person I'd want. Obviously it never came to that but Jordan's attitude when it came to that was, 'No I don't want to go, I want to fight for my place'. That's why any accolade he gets is fully and utterly deserved. His attitude, both to himself and others has always been paramount."

# CHAPTER FIVE
# SENT TO COVENTRY

Traditionally being sent to Coventry means you are ostracised and ignored. Nothing could have been further from the truth when the teenage Jordan Henderson arrived at Coventry City on loan at the end of January in 2009. At that point he had precisely 125 minutes of competitive first team playing time under his belt but in 13 games for Championship Coventry City Hendo got his first senior goal, his first international call up, played in an FA Cup quarter-final and saw his reputation blossom.

"He was just a young lad when he came to Coventry but he did make an impression and it's brilliant to see what he's gone on to do" remembers one time Liverpool goalkeeper and Coventry legend Steve Ogrizovic, who was on the Sky Blues coaching staff when Jordan came to the Ricoh Arena. 'Oggy' adds, "The one key thing is that it doesn't matter how much a player has got, you've got to have that character and determination to get the very very best and I think that right from the start you could see that Jordan had got that."

Having watched a home defeat at the hands of Cardiff City the evening before completing his loan move Henderson eagerly anticipated his bow for his new club with the sort of positivity people have come to expect from him, telling the Coventry Telegraph, "I saw the game against Cardiff and it was a bad result but you have just got to move forward and look at the next game, and hopefully we can beat Derby. The lads are not too down about the result and just looking forward to tomorrow's game. I have never been to Pride Park but hopefully I can get in the team. I am hoping to get a few games under my belt. Hopefully, if I am doing really well, I can extend my loan or get called back by Sunderland to get more games in the first team. I have come on against Chelsea and played against Blackburn so it was good experience, but I want to be playing first-team football as soon as possible."

That first team football came the following day when he lined up alongside the likes of Clinton Morrison and Freddy Eastwood away to a Derby County side desperate to get out of the bottom three and with the combative character of Robbie Savage in competition with the rookie Henderson in midfield. In front of a crowd of just under

30,000 within 16 minutes young Jordan was facing an uphill battle with his new team already 2-0 down. With what has become trademark stubbornness and industriousness Hendo refused to throw in the towel and helped his side to claw their way back into the game through a goal early in the second half from Michael Doyle, but the home side hung on to secure a first win for new manager Nigel Clough.

It was the first time Jordan had played a full game, his two previous appearances for parent club Sunderland having lasted 45 and 80 minutes. For many a young player just having played would have been enough and they would have been entirely focussed on their own game, but reflecting on his first Coventry appearance a few days later, while preparing for his home debut, the deep thinking youngster reflected in depth on his and the team's performance, "I enjoyed it. In the first half we were poor and I didn't really get on the ball that much but in the second half I thought we deserved something from the game. It's not about playing the best football, it's about getting three points really. We want a top-half finish here and maybe even the play-offs and the first 45 minutes wasn't good enough.

"We reacted well in the second half but we needed to. I didn't think I was too good myself in the first half but in the second half I got on the ball a bit more and created one or two chances and put a couple of good crosses in, which I was pleased with.

"In the past, when you are young, you are told to play good football and the result is not all-important. I think winning is just inside you and when you play first team football, it's all about the points. If you don't play too well and you get the win it's much better than playing well and losing. And as soon as you've lost one, you're looking forward to the next one and hopefully we can get the three points today against Wolves. The manager said to us at half-time that we needed to do a lot more and said that we were not working hard enough, not working as a team, not winning our fifty-fifties. I thought the lads reacted to his comments but you can't start making excuses for the first half. It's all experience and that's what I need. The manager might give us a talking to at half-time but I thought it worked. We are here to do a job and we have to do it for 90 minutes not just for 45."

The young Henderson's comments about 'winning is just inside you' and 'you can't start making excuses' show that the belief and unfailing honesty the nation has come to realise is part of the player's make-up has been there from the start.

Similarly that winning mentality as seen in the remark, "It's not about playing the best football, it's about getting three points really' came to fruition on his second appearance. It was the first win in a career that eventually would see him winning week-in week-out.

Following a first full week's training it looked as if the hard work in securing a 2-1 win over Championship leaders Wolves on Jordan's home debut was going to be undone when Sylvan Ebanks-Blake stepped up to take a last minute penalty but a save from Keiren Westwood secured Henderson's first ever win bonus. Interviewed that day in Coventry's match programme Jordan outlined how he was learning to cope with being away from home, "You have to adapt when you are on loan. It doesn't matter how long you are going to be here. I am here to work hard and do my best for Coventry and I will just keeping doing everything I can to impress."

He was certainly impressing. Marcus Hall was one of Henderson's team mates at Coventry. A former England Under 21 international Hall had two spells of over 150 games each for his home town club, over 100 of those appearances being in the Premier League, as well as playing for Stoke and Nottingham Forest. He remembers the impact Jordan made, "Early on during his loan I remember doing some shape work in training. I was left back and he was coming straight at me as a right midfielder. I was directly up against him and I was thinking, 'This lad just does not stop running'. It was ridiculous. He was just up and down up and down. It wasn't so much that he had any trickery or anything like that, it was just the motor and the attitude to never give in and always get back into the shape in a defensive way. It is kind of like what I see him doing at Liverpool in the way he will hold for Alexander-Arnold when he goes forward. His discipline with regard to football and his knowledge at such a young age really did stand out. I had nothing but admiration for the way he conducted himself. His professionalism for a young lad was really admirable. He was so enthusiastic and put everything into training. He would be all out and wanting to impress. He was coming into a team with a few older players in it and he was only a young lad with a growing reputation that he wanted to live up to. His attitude stands out more than anything for me. His willingness to work was phenomenal. Straight away after training he'd be in the gym or be in the gym before training and after training, working on his upper body to develop as a physical specimen as well as a player on the field."

Fully focussed on his future, Hendo wasn't hoping his career was going to blossom, he was actively doing all he could to make it happen, saying, " There's a couple of ways to get a chance in the first team at your own club. You can play well week-in, week-out for the reserves and your chance might come or you can go on loan into the Championship or League One and get a few first team games under your belt there. Once you've got that bit more experience you might get your chance in the Premier League.

"Coventry seems like a good club. The lads have been brilliant and everyone has made me feel really welcome. I'm staying in a hotel and it can get a bit boring but, at the end of the day, I am here to play football and it's not going to hurt for a few months to not be able to do anything outside of that.

"Football is my life – it has been since I was a little boy. It's all I've ever wanted to do so I am prepared to give up everything I've got to become a footballer – whether that's leaving home or leaving my friends. My number one priority is football. I've dreamt of this since I can remember and I have never wanted to do anything else."

With the hindsight of looking back on these comments well over a decade since they were made it is illuminating to note how the player who has become one of the most respected and decorated in the game was already talking about the sacrifices he was prepared to make to fulfil his dream. It is a model lesson for anyone in any walk of life to see how determination to work at your craft and the mental ability to not be tempted away from your goal has led to immense success. At this point however the player speaking was one who had played only three senior games in his career, just one of those for his new team, but rather than thinking he needed time to acclimatize Jordan was already talking about having settled in, "I've only been here a week, but Chris Coleman seems like a very good manager. He expects the best – like Roy Keane [Who had given Hendo his Sunderland debut] really. He expects you to give your best and to offer 100 per cent to the team. He wants to see hard work and improvement every day. I feel settled now. At first I was a little bit nervous about coming in but now I've been here a week or so, and it's great.

"I had a lot of family and friends at Derby last weekend – 10 of them! One of the lads at Sunderland came down too which was great. They will all be down for the

Wolves game too. You have to play football for yourself but there are a lot of people along the way who have helped you, like your family. There will be a lot of people here to watch me and I just want to go out and make them all proud."

Making people proud is something you feel Henderson would have done even had he not gone on to a glorious career with Liverpool and England. Simply being an honest professional, hard-working and respectful of the spirit of the game is something that should make family, friends and fans proud of you. Reaching the level Henderson has simply takes that to a stratospheric level.

Speaking to the Coventry Telegraph during his loan spell Hendo opened up on the advantage he had in having tremendously supportive parents, "My mam and dad have played a massive part in my career since I have been little, always there to support me, and they come to every game at the Ricoh to see me play. They have been brilliant parents who have always been there for me. My dad is called Brian and my mam is called Liz and they both support Sunderland. They are not season ticket holders at the Stadium of Light because I normally get them a couple of tickets. My dad usually goes to every game but they haven't been to many lately with me coming down here.

Next up after the win over Wolves was an FA Cup fifth round tie on Valentine's Day at a Blackburn Rovers side Henderson had already faced earlier in the season in the Carling (League) Cup for Sunderland. A few days before Jordan's loan was arranged Blackburn had faced Sunderland in an FA Cup tie at the Stadium of Light. The match had finished all-square with the draw for the fifth round giving Coventry a potential fifth round tie at Sunderland had the Black Cats won the replay. Had that been the case Henderson would have been unable to play but with Rovers winning through there was no such conflict of interest.

Against Wolves, the Sky Blues had escaped a last minute equaliser , but at Ewood Park there was no such luck as Christopher Samba pounced on a late goalkeeping error by Andy Marshall who had come into the side just before kick-off after illness forced Westwood out of the warm-up. The City squad had been weakened by a stomach bug that had affected several of the team but they were strong enough to come back and get themselves into a winning position having gone behind to a Roque Santa Cruz goal in only the second minute.

The replay was just as hard fought with Jordan's throw-in to Aron Gunnarsson leading to the only goal of the game by Leon Best. Henderson's full blooded tackle on Martin Olsson was the last action of a famous win over a team managed by Sam Allardyce's who would go on to include Jordan in the only England team he ever got to select.

Victory set up an FA Cup quarter-final, oddly against the only other Premier League side Jordan had played against prior to coming on loan: Chelsea. Before that however the youngster was fully focussed on Coventry's need for league points. Already with an old head on young shoulders, while he looked forward to the glamour of the cup-tie Hendo had clearly understood the footballer's mantra of, 'one game at a time' and illustrated that next time out just four days later by gleefully scoring the first goal of his career. It came at Carrow Road, a well taken first time shot from 12 yards that opened the scoring in a 2-1 win. Victory had Sky Blues supremo Coleman dreaming of reaching the play-offs just a month after Hendo arrived with his side ten points shy of the final play-off place.

Initially loaned for 28 days, all parties were happy to extend it to the end of the season. Jordan was enjoying first team football with a forthcoming cup quarter-final a bonus, Sunderland had climbed into the top half of the Premier League and were unbeaten in the league since allowing Jordan to go on loan, and Coventry were eager to keep him.

"I remember him impressing on the pitch. Everyone could see that he was going to be a very good player but the main thing was just the way he conducted himself. He was very determined , very respectful and listened to the coaches" remembers Steve Ogrizovic, " He wasn't shouting his mouth off or anything like that. He looked like someone who really wanted to learn his trade and be as good as he could possibly be."

Team-mate Marcus Hall remembers, "He was very quiet and unassuming off the field. He was very polite. He wasn't craving any attention , he just wanted to get on with it but he wasn't afraid to put demands on players on the pitch, even at such a young age. I suppose you have a bit more confidence to do that when you're at your own club because you probably grew up with some of the players but when you come to another club as a young lad and you've got older players in that team it probably takes a bit more guts and confidence to be able to do that. He definitely put demands on people. He wasn't anything ridiculous but he wasn't afraid to call people back into position if someone wasn't doing their work. You could tell in the games that he played that he got more and more confident in himself and he could think to himself, 'Yes I am good enough to play at this level quite easily and he took it from there. He was confident when he came, not over-confident or anything, just a really nice well-mannered young lad, but on the pitch he was the same but not afraid to make himself stand out and show what he was about and make it clear he was here to make a point.

Coventry City club historian Jim Brown concurs, "Jordan did very well at Coventry. Prior to his arrival the club had a series of loan players who failed to impress but despite Henderson's youth everyone could see he had ability combined with the hunger you expect to see from a young player. He played on the right and brought a lot of energy as well as quality to the side."

With his loan extended, Henderson played in a home defeat to Sheffield United who broke a 120 year old club record in remaining unbeaten for a 12th successive away league game. There was also a record for Coventry just three days later as a first ever sell-out crowd of over 31,000 attended a Sky Blues match at the Ricoh Arena for the visit of Chelsea.

The Londoners included seven of the men who Jordan had faced when making his Premier League debut at Stamford Bridge just four months earlier. One of these was Frank Lampard, like Stevie G the model modern midfielder and one the impressionable Henderson therefore faced twice in the first eleven appearances of his career. While Didier Drogba gave Guus Hiddink's side an early lead, Coventry remained competitive and it wasn't until the 72nd minute that a goal from Alex gave the prestigious visitors any breathing space.

The learning curve continued as back in the bread and butter games of the Championship defeats at Bristol City and Preston – where Jordan picked up his first ever caution – took City's losing sequence to four games. There was another booking in his next game as a scrappy 1-0 win was eked out over Doncaster leaving Jordan to recount, "It was a good three points against Doncaster when I thought the team worked hard and deserved their just rewards in the end. Having said that, I wasn't very pleased with my own performance. I thought I worked hard but I thought I could have done a lot more going forward and creating chances, so I just need to try to take the positives out of it. It is a learning curve for me and I am still enjoying the games and feel I am learning every time I play. I can only benefit from that experience. I have got a month and a half left at Coventry and I just need to keep working hard and trying to improve my game and play good football."

Although Hendo thought he had a month and a half left with Coventry in fact it was to be just a fortnight before injury curtailed his season. Before then though he had another significant step to take in what was his first season as a senior player.

Having made his debut in the Premier League for Sunderland and caught the eye with his performances for Coventry Jordan was called up for the first time by England. An international career that would see him go on to captain his country, play in a World Cup semi-final and who knows perhaps be part of a successful Euro 2021 side and beyond began in the modest surroundings of Walsall's Bank's Stadium at Under 19 level.

A meagre crowd of just 3,883 took in what was a goalless draw with the Czech Republic but one which featured Kyle Walker, Jack Rodwell, Martin Kelly and Danny Drinkwater who all went on to win full England caps in addition to Henderson. Inevitably, not everyone in coach Brian Eastick's England line-up went on to reach the heights, Henderson himself for instance being substituted by Manchester City's Andrew Tutte. He never managed a first-team game for City but went on to gain a lot of lower league experience, particularly with Bury and Rochdale.

Having trained with the Under 19 international squad at Aston Villa's facilities, Jordan was thrilled at his call-up. Typically, he was not letting it go to his head, saying, "It is the first time I have been called up for England at any level so it is a big step for my career but I cannot keep my head in the clouds. I have to keep my feet on the ground and keep working hard and doing exactly what I have been doing and I should be all right. I think the fact that I have been at Coventry playing first-team football has got me this call-up. I think I have done OK here and worked extremely hard to play every week. I am loving my football here. England have obviously taken notice and want to see what I can do, so I am grateful for that and I just want to take this chance. I am sure there will be some important people watching the game, maybe the Under-21 coach or even the first-team coach, but I just need to forget about that and just go out and play my football."

There wouldn't be much football for Jordan in the short term. That appearance against the Czech Republic would remain his solitary cap at Under 19 level. England wouldn't play again until May and by then Henderson was more familiar with the treatment table as the daily training pitch.

Ten days after entering the international stage Jordan's breakthrough season came to a crashing end. An hour into a goalless game with Reading for Coventry at the Ricoh Arena he suffered a fractured foot that curtailed his time at Coventry as the player returned to his parent club for treatment four days later.

Losing Henderson contributed to Coventry's season tailing off. Fourteenth and with games in hand at the time of his injury City slipped three places to 17th by the close of the campaign, despite all but one of their remaining games being against sides in the lower reaches of the table. Jordan missed out on up to seven more games for the Sky Blues.

Nonetheless the experience of playing regular first team football and learning about looking after himself was a major stepping stone as the boy Jordan began to turn into the man Henderson. During his time in the Midlands Jordan lived in an apartment in Leamington, quite close to Icelandic midfielder Aron Gunnarsson who he developed a friendship with. By his own admission, as he was able to cook a little himself, Hendo resisted the urge to visit Gunnarsson's place where his teammate had his mum living. "I don't tend to go round for Icelandic home cooking" Jordan told the local Coventry paper, understandably not fancying the possibility of those appalling Icelandic dishes of puffin or minke whale. Hopefully the Gunnarsson's were not serving up such dishes.

Looking back on how his time at the Ricoh Arena helped in his career, Henderson is always keen to acknowledge the benefit he gained from his stint in sky blue, remembering, "I was playing every week for a good club. They were doing very well in the Championship and I loved every minute of it. I felt it helped me progress as a player."

The positive feeling was entirely mutual as Steve Ogrizovic explains, "The club would have wanted to buy him if they could have done at the time but Sunderland weren't selling and he was way out of our range from that point of view. I've read some articles about him in the past and he's always said how much his loan at Coventry helped him. It's good from Coventry's point of view that we managed to get someone who has gone on to do so well at the highest echelon of the game after pulling on a Sky Blues shirt. I think that's what loans do. If you talk to all the top clubs that's what they want, they want young players to get a taste of different conditions. It teaches players to grow up very quickly. They maybe move away from their roots by moving away from home and mature rapidly, both regarding lifestyle issues and also being able to play football in a different environment with different players. The loan gave Jordan much needed playing experience that Sunderland couldn't give him at that time as a Premier League club. To come a level down and get that playing experience is something that I'm delighted he felt was so beneficial and it was certainly good for the football club and it's great that he's gone on to reach the heights that he has.

"Right from the start our first impressions were very good. He was only about 18 and played just over 10 games for us then he got injured but he made a very big impression in that space of time. In the games he had he played very well. It was a time when we were in the Championship and we played him a little bit wider on the right hand side. He was quick but I don't think that at that stage anybody ever thought he would ever get to the level that he has got to."

Marcus Hall isn't surprised Jordan has reached the peaks he has. He puts Hendo's success down to the player being able to maintain that unquenchable thirst for constant improvement, combined with a deep understanding of the game from a young age, "It's a difficult one isn't it ?" he ponders. " It's probably a shock to a lot of people that he's got so far and achieved so much really but with the attitude that he has he gave himself the chance. Sometimes people have that great attitude when they're young but then slack off a little bit, but he's kept going and kept going. He's had his doubters and people who criticised him at certain points but every time he's gone out and proved them wrong. You could see his mental strength and his attitude would take him far and it's to his testament how far it has taken him. He wasn't someone who was going to grab the headlines and I don't think he's ever been the kind of player to really grab the headlines, probably up until now when he's really been getting noticed for when he hasn't been in the team That's when his contribution has most been noticed because he's one of those players you miss when he's not there really and at last he's getting the credit he deserves. Everyone loves to go forward and do the bit that will get you the headline but not everyone wants to track back and get themselves in a position to help the team but he does it without wanting any praise. He does it because he drives the team on and as the years have gone on people have started to appreciate that more. I don't think he's that bothered whether he gets the appreciation or not. He knew what he is doing and would know his manager knew what he was doing and the fans who know what they're looking at know it and that's all you need really. You're always going to have people who are going to have a little dig at you but he's got the mental strength to be able to deal with that."

Clearly the Coventry perspective on the 18-year old who arrived at The Ricoh Arena as a lad who had played one and a half games but left as a player who had gained early experience and made such a positive impression is one that was like a searchlight on Jordan's future. Nothing he has done since then, in making his name with Sunderland, hitting the highest heights with Liverpool or starring for England have conflicted with what he showed in the Championship. Possessing determination and ambition in equal measure, Henderson has never veered from the path he set himself, of being as good as he possibly could be.

"You could see he was a very good talent" concludes Steve Ogrizovic, "He was really into his football. He was quite quiet actually when he came to the club but he was very determined and you just thought, 'Yes he's got what it takes with his character and mentality. He looked like he enjoyed the game, listened to what the manager and coaches were saying to him and in a short space of time he made a very good impression at Coventry, not just with the players and staff but also with the supporters. It's always great to see young players go on to better things. It's great for coaches to see young players they have helped along the way go on to be successful. That's what coaches are in the game for. There's a little bit of pride from the club's point of view so for Jordan Henderson to have had a few games for Coventry is satisfying. I'm pleased we were a good fit for him and he was a good fit for us. He's gone on to have an absolutely fantastic career.

"I wouldn't say the success he has had surprises me. It never does with a young player but it wasn't the case that you thought, 'Gosh we've got a future England captain here', or whatever. It was just that we had a player who we could see was going to be very good. His attitude and temperament were outstanding and that is sometimes the thing that separates the good from the very good. I'm sure from the short space of time that I saw him you could see that he was going to make the very very most of his career and he's certainly done that."

# CHAPTER SIX
# SEEING THE LIGHT

Returning to Sunderland from his loan with Coventry Jordan was bolstered by the first team experience he had pocketed combined with having been recognised internationally. There was frustration too as a result of the injury that had curtailed his Sky Blue adventure and gave him time in the treatment room at the Academy of Light when he wanted to be demonstrating his progress on the training pitch.

Working hard to recuperate and get himself ready for the 2009-10 season Henderson had a new manager to impress from scratch at Sunderland. Having caught the eye of the demanding Roy Keane who gave him his debut, he had then been loaned out by Ricky Sbragia who had since resigned to be succeeded by Steve Bruce. A former youth and reserve team coach in an earlier spell at Sunderland, Sbragia was always well informed about the youngsters coming through at the club. After Bruce took over in the hot seat Sbragia remained on the scene as chief scout and was able to add to the positive comments academy staff had for the new manager in advising him about the youthful talent at his disposal.

Bruce took no time at all to recognise Jordan's ability and potential and give him the opportunity to blossom, reflecting in 2020, "Jordan grabbed me from the day I walked in at Sunderland, with his personality and his attitude to work. It was pre-season and when we did the runs he would be at the front, then drop back and try and help somebody in the middle of the pack. Then by the time the run had finished he would be back around the front. You couldn't help but be impressed by that. I think he'd admit he has never been blessed with real natural ability but he's turned himself into a wonderful athlete and one who has always had this leadership quality about him. He had this will and determination from the time I met him – and the lads at the academy said the same. I don't think after I put him into the team that he ever came out of it."

Being inundated with calls from clubs wanting to take Hendo on loan only added to the positive reports Bruce was receiving from the academy staff at the club and seeing for himself. "I was full of admiration for the kid" enthused Bruce after throwing the teenager in at the deep end for a first Premier League start in the opening home game of the 2009-10 season against Chelsea. "He couldn't have wished for a more difficult opponent than being up against Ashley Cole but he stuck at it to his credit. I was delighted for him in the way he showed the right attitude. He'll learn from the game and I'm sure he's got a big future."

The match was also the manager's first home game. An ankle injury to Steed Malbranque had seen him call upon Henderson from half time onwards three days earlier as debutant Darren Bent got the goal in a 1-0 win at Bolton – just four days after Jordan had been capped at Under 20 level as a sub against Montenegro at the Hawthorns - but a Blues side with a midfield consisting of Deco, Michael Ballack, Frank Lampard and Michael Essien were a different kettle of fish under their own new manager Carlo Ancelotti. Although Bent gave Sunderland a half-time lead it was always an uphill struggle for Jordan and his team as the Blues enjoyed almost two thirds of possession, racked up a 14 -1 corner count and eventually earned a deserved 3-1 win. Henderson had run himself into the ground and was brought off to great applause with six minutes to go, being replaced by the experienced Irish international Andy Reid.

Characteristically Henderson hadn't just played a good game. Just as he belied his age on the pitch he did so afterwards, saying, "It's always disappointing to lose a game, especially at home but there were a lot of positives for the team and for me personally. We started the game quickly and pushed Chelsea back. They're one of the world's best teams though and they showed why they regularly win things because they took control of the game in the end."

While in later years, his time at Liverpool has seen Henderson most often be compared with Steven Gerrard, Jordan faced Gerrard's great competitor Frank Lampard in three of the first five games he played against Premier League clubs. Having scored the first goal to be netted while Jordan was on the pitch in a senior game, on this occasion Lampard scored his 132nd goal for the Blues, drawing level with Jimmy Greaves as joint sixth on the club's all-time scorers list he would eventually head. While Henderson has never been as prolific a scorer as Lampard – even allowing for the latter's penchant for penalties – to get a close up view of the England legend so often and so early in his time as a first teamer illustrated for Henderson the quality he had to reach to be able to live and thrive at the top level.

Playing on the right of midfield Hendo also got a close-up look at Ashley Cole. Totally undaunted by the task he noted, "It's great experience for me to play against people of that quality. He's the England left back so it was a challenge for me to give him problems but also to keep him from getting forward. I found out a couple of hours before the game that I'd be starting. There wasn't much time to be nervous. I was more excited."

Excitement wasn't exclusive to the teenager. Staff and supporters at Sunderland could see that here was a player with a combination of ability along with the right attitude. Having been heavily involved in a demanding pre-season build up Jordan was already looking comfortable in his surroundings.

A gentle start to the season's preparations had seen Jordan employed in central midfield in a 4-0 win at Darlington prior to a training camp on the Algarve. Only one game was played on the trip to Portugal, Henderson starting on the right as Portimonense were beaten 1-0. Next stop was a step up with games against Benfica and Atletico Madrid at the home of Ajax in the Amsterdam tournament.

Bruce started Hendo in the centre of the park in both matches as Benfica handed out a 2-0 defeat before Atletico were beaten by the same score. Jordan maintained his starting central berth back on UK soil when he hit the bar from long range in a 2-1 win at Celtic but as the dress rehearsals began for the start of the Premier League campaign the youngster found himself left out of the penultimate friendly at Peterborough and brought off the bench for the last 35 minutes of a draw at Hearts. However he'd made such a positive impact that Bruce had no qualms about using him as sub at Bolton on the opening day or starting him against the might of Chelsea – Jordan's full Premier League debut therefore coming against the side he'd made his debut appearance as sub against nine months earlier.

Continuing his interview following the Chelsea defeat, Jordan spoke of his ongoing learning, his confidence and most importantly of the new role Steve Bruce was giving him. In due course he would be recognised as a master of perpetual motion and positional awareness in the heart of midfield whereas in most of his development football, appearances under Roy Keane and on loan to Coventry he had predominantly played on the right. "I loved being involved with the first team in pre-season and have already learned a lot, but I've a lot more to learn" he said.

"My confidence is high and being involved with the first team training, and in games, will make me better if I keep my head down and continue to work hard. The manager gave me the chance to play in central midfield as well as on the wing during pre-season and I enjoyed that. It was a different challenge but playing against massive clubs like Benfica, Atletico Madrid and Celtic was great. I enjoyed playing through the middle but I don't mind playing wide on the right either – to be honest I don't really mind where I play as long as I'm playing. Learning a new position like central midfield can only help my career and my awareness for when I play on the wing. It means I have more to offer the manager."

Offering more to the manager is something Henderson has continued to do throughout his career. He always offers more than many people initially realise. This is because as a person who from the beginning of his career has appreciated what the team needs ultimately matters more than what looks good for him personally, Jordan's qualities are such that fellow professionals are the first to recognise his role. Part of this selflessness is a life-long awareness of the value of his team-mates. While Jordan always wanted to play and stressed he wasn't bothered where he was playing as long as he was in the team, he was always keen to acknowledge that as an up and coming player he was surrounded by more senior professionals, "If the manager tells me I'm going to be involved again that will be great and I'll do my best but we've got a strong squad and there are more experienced players around me."

Henderson's move up the pecking order was indicated by a change from being squad number 42 to 16. A couple of weeks later as the transfer window drew to a close Steve Bruce felt able to sell central midfielder Grant Leadbitter and allow Teemu Tainio to head out on a year's loan. Bruce had brought in Albania captain Lorik Cana and also recruited Lee Cattermole from Wigan, a player he had earlier taken to the Latics from Middlesbrough. Cana and England Under 21 captain Cattermole produced a combative central midfield and Sunderland went up to seventh in the Premier League, leap-frogging Liverpool after Darren Bent's infamous 'beach-ball goal' in mid-October. Henderson came off the bench in that match as he had in six of the seven league games since the Chelsea match but when Cattermole was ruled out of the next fixture at Birmingham Hendo was back in the starting line-up.

The Blues were a team Jordan had good memories of. A month earlier he had scored his first goal for his home town club in a 2-0 Carling Cup win against them at the Stadium of Light, netting after just four minutes from a Kenwyne Jones' cross. With Sunderland's record post-war goal-scorer Kevin Phillips on the pitch for the visitors, Jordan punctured the cup hopes of a player he'd grown up supporting. In another interview he'd done with me for that night's programme the teenager explained, "I've been supporting Sunderland since I was little. I used to go to Roker Park with my Dad [Roker Park closed when Jordan was seven] so to grow up watching Sunderland and now be part of the team is great."

"I've been over the moon to have been involved so much" he continued, "My target before the season was to be involved with the first team squad a lot more regularly and obviously I've been doing that so far."

By this time manager Bruce was already on record speaking of how impressed he was with his young midfielder. This was music to Jordan's ears, albeit Bruce wouldn't deliver his praise in the sort of Rap Hendo was listening to at the time, "It means a lot. The gaffer's given me a chance to get a lot of experience since he's been at the club already and it gives me confidence when he says things like he has. I have definitely improved over the last year on the technical side. When I went to Coventry my knowledge of the game obviously improved. I played a lot of first team football there and it's helped for when I've come back.

I've just been enjoying my football. I think that's the main thing – the enjoyment of football and if you are enjoying your football other positive things come along with it."

Things were happening quickly for Jordan at this point. His performances were being noticed by one and all. Chairman Niall Quinn remarked, "He's a great kid who is an absolute credit to his family and the fans already love him because he is one of their own. I was delighted to have his mam, dad and the rest of his family up to the Board room afterwards [After his first goal] for a celebratory drink. His parents must be very proud of him and they must take credit for the fact they have a great young man on their hands." Quinn's joy with Jordan was unbridled as he continued, "He plays with a lovely big smile on his face because he is so happy to be where he is and to be doing what he's doing. His energy levels are incredible and it's satisfying to be able to enjoy it when success like this happens to a good kid who looks out for the other young players at the club. He's a terrific example and is a leader already."

On Wearside Quinn has Messianic status and these words were certainly prophetic but he wasn't the only good judge to be noticing a player who would go on to the successes Jordan has had and will continue to have. Three days before his goal against Birmingham he had come off the bench for the final 15 minutes of a Premier League defeat at Burnley. It was sufficient for the highly respected former England international Jimmy Armfield, summarising for BBC Radio 5 live, to tell me in the press room afterwards, "He looks a good player that lad. I was really impressed with him."

Sunderland skipper Lorik Cana needed no prompting to add to the showering of praise on the youngster after being seen to hand out some Jurgen Klopp style advice on the pitch, "Some people noticed me at one point putting my arm around Jordan Henderson to talk to him. It is important when you see he is a player who has a lot of quality and is a fantastic player. I think he is maybe going to be one of the best midfield players in England in future so he has to learn a lot because he is young. I am really happy for him especially as he scored and showed to the manager and everyone that he can play and of course I am trying to help him a lot because he has to learn all the time but he wants to learn and has a good mentality." Albania's most capped international, Cana played for PSG, Marseille, Galatasaray, Lazio and Nantes as well as Sunderland. A deep thinker who since hanging up his boots has been appointed the Honorary Ambassador for Kosovo, Cana was the first professional to not just say they were impressed with Henderson's attitude and ability but to publicly predict a future as one of the best midfielders in England.

There was still plenty of work to do of course. That full Premier League away debut at St. Andrews saw Jordan be one of three midfielders taken off as part of a triple substitution mid-way through the second half in a 2-1 defeat. There was another disappointment in midweek when he showed the bottle to step up to take a penalty in a Carling Cup shoot-out with Aston Villa only for Brad Guzan to save his spot-kick, Henderson being the third of four Sunderland players to fail from the spot after a goalless draw in which Sunderland had missed another penalty in normal time.

Never an assured penalty taker, as well as missing one for Liverpool in the pre-season Audi Cup final in 2016 more notably he also failed to score for England in the World Cup win over Columbia in 2018. More often than not Jordan won't be spotted in the first five penalty shoot-out takers but as can be seen from him stepping up against Columbia – when he was amongst the senior players in the team – he is prepared to take responsibility.

The learning continued in his Sunderland days as the back to back losses to Birmingham and Villa signalled the start of the first bad run of Henderson's career. Just two of 21 games would be won – one against non-league Barrow in the FA Cup – but while the team struggled Jordan maintained his industry and commitment while showing he had the quality to not be out of place in the Premier League.

During this run Jordan had scored his first Premier League goal just before Christmas but the fact it came in a match where Sunderland scored three times and still lost illustrates the difficulties Steve Bruce was having, even allowing for the fact the 4-3 defeat was at Manchester City on a day when City sacked manager Mark Hughes straight after the game. Jordan's goal bore a strong resemblance to the goal he scored for Coventry, hit first time and right-footed from similar distance to his goal for the Sky Blues at Norwich. Jordan's goal in Manchester made the score 2-2 after City had led 2-0. After the home side re-took the lead Hendo made the assist for Kenwyne Jones to head another equaliser, this time Jordan surging into space on the right, looking up and picking out his centre-forward with an inch perfect cross.

Shortly before Sunderland's sickly run ended in March Hendo damaged ankle ligaments in a draw with Wigan. Expected to be out for six weeks Jordan came back a week early, returning as a sub in the return with Manchester City and coming off the bench again against Birmingham as four points were gleaned. "It's great to be back" he said after the home draw with Manchester City but he was taking nothing for granted after the winless run had ended a few days earlier as Darren Bent bagged a mid-week hat-trick against Bolton. "I've loved this season and I've learned so much from the coaches and players here. The team have been doing well without me so I expect it will be hard to get back in."

Despite his modesty – never a false modesty – Henderson was quickly restored to the starting line-up and stayed there until the end of the season as Bruce steered his side to 13th place, the club's highest ranking since being promoted three years earlier. This late run included a first appearance at Anfield. Taking an early lead Liverpool dominated, winning 3-0 with two of the goals coming from Fernando Torres. As Sunderland scrambled to restrict Liverpool only the most astute home fans might have realised that the teenager working his socks off to stem the red tide would one day be a Champions League winning Liverpool captain, but Henderson typically never gave up and managed a couple of shots before giving way to Liverpool old boy Bolo Zenden for the last 12 minutes.

Despite missing some of the season through injury Henderson had played in 33 Premier League games, 23 of those as starts. Only once had he been available and not played, on that occasion as an unused sub in a big early season win over Hull. Only ever- present Darren Bent played in more top-flight games than Jordan who ended the season still a teenager and not surprisingly been named Sunderland's Young Player of the Year. "The fans have been great all the way through. It's a great honour to get the award from them and that gives me even more confidence" remarked a player delighted with the award and also with a new five-year contract he had been given along with fellow young midfielder David Meyler. "It's great for David and I" beamed Jordan who would often be spotted in Amore, a classy but quiet and out of the way Italian restaurant in a basement in a less than salubrious part of town. "We're good mates and we love playing football. Whether it's training or a game at the weekend we will give it 100 per cent. The club offered me five years which I was very happy about. I need to prove now that they were right to do that - keep doing the right things and hopefully get better. The club always said if I was doing well they would reward me and they have done that. I've only been in the first team one season so I certainly don't think I've cracked it and can relax. I'd be daft to think that. Next year will be a big challenge to see if I can push on even more. I have the right people around me to keep my feet on the ground and I'm confident I can improve."

Never a 'showy' player Henderson has always focussed on doing what was most effective which is not always the same thing as the most eye-catching. Football is littered with stylish players able to make a crowd ooh and aah while defenders get back into position. Henderson will retain possession if a penetrating ball is not on but if a defence splitting pass is there to be played he has always possessed the vision to see it and the technique to deliver it. However during this first season as a Premier League regular he had developed a trade-mark of nut-megging a defender, getting to the by-line and whipping a ball in. This wasn't arrogance so much as the vitality of youth simply looking to get the better of an opponent. When he did it to Paul Scholes in the last home match of the season though it illustrated that no matter who the opposition, to Jordan they were just another opponent. When asked if he was ever fazed about playing against the very best he instantly responded, "I don't think you can be. You have to give respect to top players but once a game starts everyone is equal and you have to have confidence and show what you can do."

Jordan was in reflective mood when he spoke to me an in-depth end of season interview for the club magazine, Legion of Light, "It's been a brilliant season and I've loved every minute of it" he said. Every game I've played I've enjoyed and I've learned from every training session and gained a little bit more experience with every game. I want to take that into next season and keep trying to improve. There are a few games that stand out as team highlights such as beating Arsenal and Liverpool at home and playing so well in getting a draw at Manchester United. For me the highlight was away to Man City where I scored my first Premier League goal. I'd scored before in the Carling Cup against Birmingham but a goal in the Premier League was more important. The cup goal was my first one but the league one was special."

Never one for resting on his laurels, as always Jordan was keener to look forward than back. Reviewing what had gone before only being of interest to him if he could use it to learn how he might improve. Just as teams sometimes come into the Premier League and initially impress only to subsequently struggle with second season syndrome, it is not unusual for young players to have outstanding breakthrough seasons and then fail to maintain the same standard as a level of expectation becomes associated with them. Without accepting any negative thoughts, Hendo was already one step ahead of any nay-sayers and was focussing on continuing his rise in the game. "I think next season is an even bigger challenge for me. I think a lot of people will be looking to see if I can have another good season and I hope if I keep working hard I can improve on the season I've just had."

Leaving his teenage years behind on the day the fixtures were published for the 2010-11 campaign Jordan was now seen as a key part of the Black Cats line up rather than a potential player who might break through. Clearly he still had a lot to learn but his energy and drive were there for all to see. His ability to perform with his head up so he could see the play marked him out as a young footballer who would go even further than his pin-point long diagonal passes.

Just four days before the first match of the season there was another confidence boost for Jordan as he made his England under 21 debut against Uzbekistan in a friendly at Bristol City's Ashton Gate. The opening day of the season saw Sunderland field half a dozen debutants on in a home draw with Birmingham but there was still a place in the starting line-up for Henderson alongside new goalkeeper Simon Mignolet who he would later be reunited with at Anfield. Also joining Jordan in the Wearsiders squad were Paraguay midfielder Cristian Riveros, just back from the World Cup and Danny Welbeck who arrived on loan from Manchester United. Welbeck and Henderson had made their Under 18 debuts for their respective clubs in the same game against each other a little over four years earlier and would go on to play together for England under two years later.

Welbeck hadn't been signed in time to feature in the pre-season build up which saw Jordan play against a Munster XI in Limerick, Darlington at what has become the white elephant of a gorgeous stadium built by George Reynolds (who was later jailed for tax evasion), then three games on the Algarve at Albufiera against fellow tourists Brighton and Hull before a meeting with Benfica. Back in England Jordan got the winner in a friendly away to Leicester before playing in the final warm-up match which was lost away to Bundesliga outfit 1899 Hoffenheim.

It was the curtain raiser to what would be Jordan's last season before leaving his home town team for Liverpool. Now wearing number 10 Jordan went on to play more than anyone in the squad – something that would become a familiar part of his story. He started every game but one, being left out as an unused sub in a home game against West Brom in April following a 5-0 thrashing at Manchester City.

The opening part of the season saw Henderson impress as Manchester City were defeated at the Stadium of Light. It was the only victory in the opening eight games.

Six of these were drawn including a match at Anfield where Liverpool were rescued by a late header from Steven Gerrard. With Henderson's energy and crisp passing at the forefront Sunderland had come from behind to lead with a Darren Bent brace. The Wearsiders had been aggrieved at Liverpool's fifth minute opening goal. Centre back Michael Turner had nonchalantly back-heeled the ball towards goalkeeper Mignolet for him to take a free-kick only for Fernando Torres to race in and play the ball to Dirk Kuyt who scored. When referee Stuart Attwell allowed the goal to stand Sunderland felt as if they'd failed to pay someone to look after their car, not least as any doubt as to whether Turner had actually 'taken' the free-kick should have been overridden by Torres having not been ten yards away. "Even the dogs in the street knew what had really happened" asserted Niall Quinn.

Liverpool's fans were no happier, many staying behind after the final whistle to protest against American owners Tom Hicks and George Gillett as Hendo waved at the Sunderland fans before disappearing down the tunnel unaware that the media storm surrounding the game's controversies would be of no concern to the man busy noting how well the 20-year old Henderson had played: England coach Franco Baldini.

Having broken into the national Under 21 team at the beginning of the season, by this time Henderson had added two further caps in the UEFA Under 21 championship 2011 preliminaries. He impressed in a 1-0 win in Portugal and a straightforward 3-0 victory over Lithuania in Colchester. In Portugal his future Liverpool team-mate Daniel Sturridge got the goal while his current Sunderland colleague Danny Welbeck got a couple of goals against the Lithuanians.

After one more club game in which he impressed in a home draw with Manchester United Hendo was back in an England shirt. Having already had good reports on the 20-year old England manager Fabio Capello travelled to Carrow Road to see the first leg of a play-off game for the Under 21 championships with Romania. It was to be a great night for England and for Jordan. On the ground where Hendo had scored the first senior goal of his career while on loan to Coventry he scored a beauty to register his first goal while sporting the three lions. Having earlier seen a cracking volley tipped over Jordan scored the first goal in a 2-1 win with another superb volley from outside the box. He met a punched clearance from a Tom Cleverley corner, showing immaculate technique to ping the ball into the bottom corner. Keeping his eye on the dipping ball despite approaching defenders who could have clattered him, he didn't take the leather off the ball but controlled the shot brilliantly to hit the target. Allied to another all action display of industry and quality Henderson gave Capello plenty to think about and after helping the Under 21s to a goalless draw in the second leg four days later in Botosani he would find that next time the Under 21s were in action he wasn't involved – as he'd been called up by Capello for the full squad.

Following the international break Henderson slotted straight back into his Sunderland side that climbed up to seventh in the Premier League after taking four points from their next two games. Then came the chastening derby at Newcastle that led to the training ground reaction that was the tipping point in Damien Comolli deciding to exceed his budget to capture Hendo's signature for Liverpool (as outlined in the 'Never Replace Stevie G' chapter).

Responding to the heavy derby defeat Asamoah Gyan hit the goals trail. Jordan had supplied a magnificent assist as the Ghana striker marked his debut in English football with a goal at Wigan in early September but Gyan hadn't scored since. He put that right with two goals to beat Stoke and grabbed another in a mid-week at Spurs before Sunderland rolled up at Stamford Bridge on the weekend before the next batch of internationals.

Already five points clear at the top of the Premier League with a 100% home record and having gone 916 minutes without conceding at the Bridge the Blues were dismantled by Sunderland who won 3-0. The opening goal, a beautiful slaloming run from Nedum Onuoha, came when a Henderson cross was cleared while the second from Gyan came from a first time Hendo pass after a typically intelligent run from the youngster who spotted the chance to join in a slick attack.

Having been impressed when seeing Jordan in action at Tottenham, if Capello had any doubts about blooding Henderson in a Wembley Friendly with France, the performance he witnessed against his fellow Italian Carlo Ancelotti's side evidently made his mind up as three days later Henderson was back in the capital starting for the national team. Lining up alongside Steven Gerrard, Jordan was the second youngest player to start the game, nine days older than France midfielder Yann M'Vila who would later play for Sunderland too.

Never a dirty player, Henderson picked up the game's only yellow card for a foul on Lyon's Yoann Gourcuff early in the second half. Capello used six substitutes as England lost 2-1 but had the faith in Henderson to leave him on for the full 90 minutes with Hendo explaining, "Fabio Capello just said, 'Well done' and asked me if it was different? I said 'Yes it was a little bit' and he told me 'Go back and play for your club and keep doing what I'd been doing."

Club manager Steve Bruce, "Told me not to let the game or the result knock me and to just keep going, do what I've been doing and take the experience on board." Surprisingly Bruce never won a full international cap but Jordan's chairman won 92 of them and as ever Niall Quinn accentuated the positive. As Henderson was making his England debut Niall was watching Brazil take on Argentina in Qatar having travelled to Doha to make a presentation on behalf of Sunderland AFC's thriving charity then called the Sunderland Foundation. Watching the big South American clash Quinn observed, "Chelsea's Ramires was the main player. I reminded myself that just three days earlier Jordan Henderson had given him the run-around at Stamford Bridge."

Having had a taste of elite level international football Jordan would not get another full cap for 18 months by which time he was at Liverpool and Capello had been replaced by Roy Hodgson. Undaunted, Henderson did what both Capello and Bruce advised which was to keep on keeping on at club level, which he did while continuing his international education with the Under 21s.

Three games later he scored the winner against West Ham and continued to consistently impress as he played a major role in maintaining Sunderland in the top six until February. Shortly after the sudden departure of Darren Bent during the January transfer window the team lost their cutting edge and plummeted to 15th before the late season arrival of Bruce's former club Wigan.

With Sunderland going in the wrong direction the meeting with the Latics, who were one place above the drop zone and four points behind the Wearsiders, was a key game. Bruce's men needed to arrest their decline which had brought just a solitary point from nine matches.

That decline looked like continuing when a thunderbolt from Mo Diame put Wigan ahead six minutes into the second half in front of 39,000 anxious fans.

Asamoah Gyan quickly equalised but was then stretchered off leaving an already injury hit team without a recognised striker. Having spent most of the campaign in central midfield Jordan had reverted to a wide right position three games earlier and had recently been left out of the side for the only time in the entire campaign, as harsher critics grumbled he looked jaded and questioned his ability to be a goal threat.

What was never in doubt was his commitment and willingness to solve any problem by working as hard as he could, never letting the team down through lack of effort. Rather than going into a shell and feeling sorry for himself, hiding and not wanting the ball, Henderson showed the mental toughness all top players need and played himself through this tough spell.

On this occasion Jordan stepped forward to score the first senior brace of his career to inspire his team to a much needed 4-2 victory. Playing a ball out wide he burst through the middle to get on the end of the incoming cross from Sulley Muntari and put his side ahead with a left-footed drive before scoring again 11 minutes later, this time taking a touch before clinically despatching his shot having received from Stephane Sessegnon.

There would be just four more appearances for his first club. The last of these at already relegated West Ham saw him sign off with the cross that produced the last goal of the season as Riveros registered his only goal in English football on what was also his last game.

Having been named his club's Young Player of the Year for the third season running Hendo had played 79 games for Sunderland, including 12 as sub, scoring five goals. In 31 months since his debut, by this time as he approached his 21st birthday Jordan had a full England cap to his name and the European Under 21 Championships to look forward to in the summer. These would take place in Denmark where he had returned to the England Under 21 line-up with the last goal in a 4-0 friendly win five days after playing against Liverpool at the Stadium of Light in March. By the time he got to these he would be representing England as a Liverpool player.

## CHAPTER SEVEN

# OLD HEAD TO LEARN FROM

Twenty two points. That was the gap between sixth placed Liverpool and Premier League champions Manchester United as Sir Alex Ferguson's Red Devils' claimed a 19th league title overall in the summer of 2011, thereby drawing level with Liverpool on the all-time honours board. It was also a 12th Premier League crown for the Old Trafford club while Kenny Dalglish's Anfield side were mere also rans. Liverpool failed to even qualify for the Europa League as their supporters continued to crave the Holy Grail of the Premier League title that had never come to Merseyside.

As the dust settled on a campaign that had brought Liverpool third round exits in both domestic cup competitions and a round of 16 Europa League elimination to Portuguese side Braga envious eyes were cast on the five clubs above them. Champions Manchester United had reached the Champions League final against Barcelona at Wembley. Runners' up Chelsea and fifth placed Spurs had progressed as far as the Champions League quarter-finals, third placed Manchester City had won the FA Cup and fourth placed Arsenal had reached the League Cup final. Liverpool had to settle for finishing one place above Everton.

Work needed doing. For the club where the iconic Bill Shankly said, "If you are first you are first. If you are second you are nothing," sixth was nowhere – except it was one place higher than Liverpool had managed the year before.

Club legend Kenny Dalglish was preparing for his first full season back in charge at Anfield. He had taken over in January following the departure of Roy Hodgson. Future England manager Hodgson had arrived in the summer to replace Rafa Benitez. A club with success based on stability had therefore had as many managers in seven months as they had numbered in the previous 17 years, since Roy Evans replaced Graeme Souness. The much travelled Hodgson had arrived from an impressive spell with Fulham, signing a three-year contract which turned out to last just seven months

Hodgson had wheeled and dealed in the summer, chief amongst the departures being Javier Mascherano to Barcelona for £18.5m. Coming through the in-door the most expensive purchase had been the £11.5m capture of Raul Meireles from Porto. Amongst the other arrivals were Joe Cole on a free from Chelsea and the £1.7m acquisition of Charlton's Jonjo Shelvey, a player who had first crossed paths with future signing Jordan Henderson in the FA Youth Cup.

Astonishingly after eight games Liverpool were joint bottom, the middle of three teams on six points. In the League Cup Hodgson's hotch-potch had been bundled out at Anfield on penalties...by Northampton Town. Three days later a late Stevie G equaliser earned a point at home to a Henderson propelled Sunderland.

Troubled times on the pitch reflected a turbulent period off it with Barclays Bank seeking a buyer for the club as behind the scenes directors ended up in the High Court.

Mascherano had apparently refused to play at Manchester City as he looked to secure his transfer to Barca while in the background moves to sell the club gathered pace. With a mid-October deadline to repay a loan apparently totalling £237m to the Royal Bank of Scotland looming, even the future of the club was in question.

Eventually the new owners that would become Fenway Sports Group gained control after a truly tumultuous period in the history of the club. Meanwhile, the experienced Hodgson tried to affect an improvement on the pitch while outgoing owners Tom Hicks and George Gillett wrangled over the sale of Liverpool F.C.

Despite that eighth Premier League result (which saw Liverpool in 19th place) coming in a 2-0 defeat at Everton those who had walked through a storm looked for a golden sky as a new dawn for the club emerged. With the future looking more settled three successive wins speedily propelled the Reds into the top half of the table. They remained there as 2010 turned into 2011 before being well beaten at Blackburn in what would be Hodgson's last stand before he left the club by mutual consent. His penultimate home game had seen his substitution of David N'Gog for Ryan Babel jeered while the substitution of his signing Paul Konchesky was cheered. Bottom of the table Wolves had picked up just one point away from Molineux all season but won at Anfield as home fans chanted for Dalglish.

Their wish was granted within days and with the January transfer window already open a flurry of activity at the end of the month produced some of the glitz and glamour that the signing of Henderson in the summer would fail to match.

The final day of King Kenny's first transfer window saw over £100m of transfer activity. The £50m sale of wantaway goal machine Fernando Torres to Chelsea was accompanied by a club record £22.8m spent on Luis Suarez from Ajax. That record that was broken just a few hours later when Newcastle United held out for a whopping £35m for England striker Andy Carroll. It was the sort of deadline day drama that had Sky Sports in meltdown and Liverpool fans the world over feeling a mixture of disappointment and delight as the spearhead of the team transformed.

Within a week of the transfer window closing Liverpool had climbed to sixth following a win at Torres' Chelsea. Carroll was not involved. He had arrived injured, wouldn't debut until March and would score in just one Liverpool game up to the end of the season. Born around ten miles away from Henderson's birthplace, under a year before Jordan was born, Carroll's six Premier League goals cost Liverpool just under £6m each. He was eventually sold to West Ham for a £20m loss after his first full season when the Tynesider was joined by Wearsider Henderson.

Given the furore in some quarters over the £16.75m subsequently spent on Henderson compared to the money lavished on a striker who had all the assets to make him worth that investment but failed to deliver Hendo looks like a bargain. Suarez on the other hand came off the bench to score in a home win over Stoke just two days after arriving and developed into Liverpool's main man with his appetite for the ball, the headlines and getting on the score-sheet, something he did on the last occasion Henderson played against Liverpool, at the Stadium of Light in March.

Despite losing at Roy Hodgson's West Brom in April as well as losing the last couple of games Liverpool finished sixth, those closing defeats extinguishing hopes of European qualification. While sixth was a position nowhere near good enough for fans reared on believing second was nothing it was a marked improvement on being joint bottom. Dalglish had re-invigorated the team with a licence to attack in contrast to the safety first tactics seen earlier in the season. Gates had slumped to almost 10,000 below capacity in the Premier League before the turnaround but as the summer of 2011 approached fans could eagerly look to the team strengthening under the new owners who had broken the club record fee twice on the last day of the previous transfer window.

Twenty days after the curtain came down on the season with a defeat at Aston Villa Reds supporters got their first 'done-deal' of the summer. Amidst the usual round of media speculation as to who would come in to bolster Liverpool's latest attempt to re-join the leading pack supporters were looking for a star name to add class and vitality to their improving line up.

When the first signing of the summer was revealed as a twenty year old from Sunderland keyboard warriors were quick to criticise. "Can't tackle and bottles 50-50 balls" declared a Neil David Harrop who can't have seen Henderson play given Jordan has never bottled anything on a football pitch since he first stepped on one. "That's a brilliant signing for Liverpool, NOT" commented a Graeme Cummins sarcastically while Chris Maisey said: "What a rip off, just like Andy Carroll. I'm sure he will suck just as bad." Perhaps those supporters now feel Liverpool have had value for money for the player Dalglish showed faith in when Jordan was only 20. Likewise another supporter, Julian Hudson hoped he would be proved wrong when taking to social media arguing of Henderson's transfer, "This sums up everything wrong with our game. At least Carroll has obvious potential and may well prove the doubters wrong, but Henderson? I feel sorry for him - the pressure on him to deliver may will destroy him. I hope I am wrong."

Hudson was right that Henderson would come under pressure. Plenty were ready to criticise. In professional football you can have all the talent in the world but if you don't have the mental strength to cope with criticism you will get nowhere. One of Henderson's greatest assets is his single-minded ability to use criticism as a motivational tool, an 'I'll show you attitude.' Taking flak from fans is part of a footballer's normal experience. It is the manager's opinion that counts but even when his future at Liverpool was under threat as Brendan Rodgers looked to move him on Henderson's stubbornness shone through. He simply dug in his heels and resolved to prove to his boss that the contribution he had to make was one the club could not afford to throw away.

As Jordan signed for Liverpool the number one single in the UK, appropriately enough, was 'Give Me Everything' by Pitbull. Whatever criticism anyone might have of Henderson no-one is able to criticise Jordan for not giving everything every time.

It was a slow start for the youthful newcomer in pre-season. After not featuring on a warm-up tour of China Henderson began in the more familiar surroundings of Hull. Being substituted in a friendly is not necessarily indicative of not playing well as managers look to build up the fitness of their squad, but being on the wrong end of a 3-0 mauling by the Tigers was an inauspicious start. Hendo then missed out on a game with Galatasaray in Istanbul and had a quiet time wide on the right in the final two rehearsals. The first of these saw a 3-3 draw with Valerenga in Oslo where the game was preceded by a minute's silence due to horrendous attacks in Norway on 22 July that saw 77 innocent people killed by a terrorist. Jordan tried to support Kuyt who was up front with Carroll in that match without much joy and there was little more to be found as he made his bow at Anfield against Valencia.

The arrival of Valencia gave home support their first viewing of the £47m worth of investment Liverpool had made into their midfield. With Luis Suarez not yet returned from Copa America duty with Uruguay Alberto Aquilani played off target man Andy Carroll. The strikers were to be supported by a midfield that had local lad Jay Spearing partnered in the centre with £6.75m newcomer Charlie Adam. He was a player they had attempted to sign in the previous transfer window but were now able to acquire with an increased bid following Adam's club Blackpool's relegation. Starting on the left and with a view to supplying the ammunition for Carroll to destroy defences was England winger Stewart Downing. He had arrived during the summer from Villa for an undisclosed fee, but one widely believed to be in the region of £20m.

Completing the Liverpool midfield was Henderson on the right hand side. Reported to have cost £16.75m, with potential add-ons taking the total price to £20m, for that outlay he was expected to instantly deliver rather than go into the 'one for the future' category. Unable to get into the game as Valencia were beaten 2-0 Henderson didn't look to have done enough to warrant a place in the starting XI for the big Premier League kick-off the following weekend when crowd favourite Dirk Kuyt was widely expected to get the nod to take up the right flank berth.

Instead as Henderson's former team mates from Sunderland walked past the, 'This is Anfield' sign to kick off the new season Kuyt made his way to the bench as Henderson lined up. With Steven Gerrard ruled out with a groin strain Hendo had Lucas Leiva for company in the engine room alongside Adam and Downing. Behind him Jordan had a player even younger than him, 18-year old Jon Flanagan but there was know-how and experience in central defence where Jamie Carragher partnered Daniel Agger, with Jose Enrique at left-back. The Spaniard was another newcomer from the north east having arrived from Newcastle for £7m just 48 hours earlier. Completing Dalglish's selection Enrique's countryman Pepe Reina was in goal, while up front Henderson and co were looking to find January joiners Andy Carroll and Luis Suarez.

As always on a debut players are eager to impress their new manager and new fans. Already having underwhelmed Liverpool's vast fan-base with his arrival Henderson found himself overshadowed as Anfield regulars warmed more to Jordan's fellow new midfielders. Charlie Adam shifted straight into top gear, stroking the ball around with such confidence and composure he could still have been sporting tangerine at the seaside. It took the Scottish schemer just 12 minutes to register his first assist as Suarez made up for an early penalty miss by capitalising on Adam's astute dead-ball to open the scoring. With some tangible reward visible for his efforts Adam controlled the game, drawing murmurings of approval from his new followers every time he drove a rapier like pass to a colleague in red.

While Adam had an assist under his belt within quarter of an hour Stewart Downing would register neither an assist nor a goal in his entire first term, yet he was desperately unlucky not to get off the mark before his first half-time team-talk as a Liverpool player. 34 minutes had elapsed when he saw a blistering shot skim off the bar after one of his trademark slaloming runs that had seen him slide past a series of despairing defenders.

With Henderson having done nothing of note other than run around a lot, when the first interval pies and pints of the season were served up the talk was about the new-men from Blackpool and Villa. It certainly wasn't the debut Hendo would have hoped for as on the hour mark he was replaced by Kuyt three minutes after Sunderland equalised with a spectacular volley from Sweden international, Seb Larsson, one of the players signed to replace him.

Plenty were ready to use social media and message boards to confirm their own comments about the wisdom or otherwise of spending such a large fee on

Henderson. "Mid-table material' and 'Still not convinced by Henderson' being amongst the kinder initial comments. Despite a well-taken goal in the next home game as Liverpool beat Bolton Wanderers to go top of the embryonic Premier League table many remained unimpressed by the expensive young signing who appeared to have stamina rather than skill as his main asset.

Liverpool didn't have long to acclimatise to being top of the table, albeit by a single goal on goal difference. Within 24 hours they trailed the Manchester clubs by a couple of points as they maintained their 100% starts in scintillating style, United thrashing Arsenal 8-2 at Old Trafford while City went to White Hart Lane and defeated Tottenham 5-1. By the time Liverpool went to Spurs a couple of games later the chasm between the men from Anfield and the elite was highlighted. Rather than winning by four goals at the Lane they lost by that margin, ending the game in disarray having been reduced to nine men with the dismissals of Charlie Adam and Martin Skrtel.

The third home game would mark the return from injury of Stevie G, but still struggling to capture the imagination Jordan had been hooked ten minutes before Gerrard's 82nd minute introduction, Kuyt once again coming on to offer more excitement and attacking threat.

With the Merseyside derby against Everton at Goodison Park next up Henderson's slow start saw him benched for the first time, Kuyt getting the nod although at 0-0 he fluffed a penalty saved by Tim Howard. With Everton down to 10 men following the controversial dismissal of Jack Rodwell mid-way through the first half, Liverpool eventually wore their weakened opponents down. They broke the deadlock with under 20 minutes to go and doubled the lead with eight minutes left, but it wasn't until the final couple of minutes that Henderson was called upon to make a blink and you'll miss it appearance.

Jordan stayed on the bench for the next couple of Premier League games. With Gerrard fit again and restored to the starting line up the chances of the young midfielder quickly regaining his Premier League place didn't look promising. Being selected to start the next game was a double-edged sword. Having been left out of Liverpool's opening two Carling Cup games of the season Jordan found himself called upon to start in the same competition at Stoke.

It was a timely opportunity as having fallen behind to a goal by his old Sunderland team-mate Kenwyne Jones, Henderson's never say die attitude had an opportunity to come to the fore. Liverpool came back to win, Suarez heading a late winner from a clever volleyed cross from Hendo. The performance shunted Jordan back into favour. Dalglish's team took four points without conceding a goal against WBA and Swansea with Hendo in the starting XI but Jordan was back on the bench when Liverpool faced a stiffer test against Chelsea at Stamford Bridge. He was the first man King Kenny turned to when he made his first change of an edgy game, young Jordan coming on for Craig Bellamy with the score tied at one-all. With five minutes left a determined run by Henderson created an opening where Kuyt missed the target having been fed by Downing, but before Dalglish's anguish had subsided Liverpool snatched the game with a terrific strike from Glen Johnson.

Having done enough to regain his place in the starting line-up Hendo would stay there for the next 11 Premier League fixtures. Even after being ruled out of a home goalless draw with Spurs his increasing value to the side was recognised when he was immediately restored to the starting line-up for a trip to Manchester United where Liverpool lost 2-1. That match was overshadowed by Luis Suarez's first meeting with Patrice Evra, for whom he had been punished with an eight game suspension after being found guilty of racially abusing Evra in their previous meeting.

Better times were ahead in cup competitions if not the league. A week after returning at Old Trafford Jordan played his part in an easy 6-1 home win over a shambolic Brighton who scored three own-goals as Liverpool marched into the FA Cup quarter-finals. Liverpool would go on to reach the final but first they had the League Cup final to contest with Cardiff City at Wembley.

Malky Mackay's Bluebirds took Liverpool all the way to penalties with Liverpool holding their nerve to win after missing their first two spot-kicks, Steven Gerrard's cousin Anthony failing with the final kick for the Welsh underdogs. Hendo had to watch the denouement having been subbed just shy of the hour mark, a couple of minutes before Liverpool levelled. Nonetheless it was a first senior medal for Jordan and tangible reward for his first campaign with Liverpool.

Having silverware to show for Kenny Dalglish's return was welcome, regardless of it being a trophy that in more successful times Liverpool would look upon as a poor relation. However it couldn't mask a shocking run as Liverpool lost six out of seven league games. Only a home victory over Everton compensated for a barren run that included Jordan's first return to his old club Sunderland, a game where his hoped for successful return saw him substituted.

His return to the north east three weeks later would see Hendo be a substitute rather than substituted in a defeat at Newcastle and while cup progress continued towards another Wembley final Liverpool's league showing was decidedly second rate. With nine of the last 14 Premier fixtures lost and a final position of eighth being a decline on the previous campaign's disappointment, and their joint lowest since 1994, it was no surprise that despite his iconic status King Kenny was deposed.

The FA Cup final had been lost to Chelsea with many Liverpool fans quick to question Henderson's contribution regardless of him scoring his second goal of the season three days after Wembley when Chelsea were defeated 4-1 at Anfield in what was Dalglish's send off.

Three days after the curtain came down on the season with a toothless 1-0 defeat at Swansea, where Danny Graham's late winner was his 100th league goal, came the news of Dalglish's departure. Although Liverpool had reached two finals and won a trophy in what was Dalglish's only full season of his second spell in charge at Anfield his spending in the transfer market was one of the factors that apparently counted against him. He had invested in English talent with big money buys in Carroll, Downing and Henderson, none of whom had set the world alight, although for a player who was still only 21 as the season closed Henderson had actually done better than most gave him credit for.

Hendo may not have been the commandingly influential player people came to recognise by the end of the decade but he had made more appearances than anyone at the club – playing in 48 out of 51 matches and being named Liverpool's Young Player of the Season. That is not a record to be sniffed at for a young player coming into as big a club as Liverpool. He also had already shown the leadership qualities which would become key to the club's success.

Ultimately Henderson's fellow north-easterners Carroll and Downing didn't do themselves justice on Merseyside but perhaps more might have come from them had Dalglish been given the opportunity to develop the side in the fashion he envisaged. Former Liverpool managing director Christian Purslow felt that Dalglish's departure was premature, telling BBC Radio 5 Live that, "They invested a lot of money in his team and I'm not sure they've given him anywhere near enough time to make the investment work."

Despite the doubters of the time, Dalglish has undoubtedly been proved right with his acquisition of Henderson. Hardly surprisingly Hendo remains indebted to the manager who backed his judgement in sanctioning his signing, "He always had your back – publicly and privately. He would stand up for you when others were critical and would always be in your corner" Jordan explained to Liverpool's official website in 2017. "He wanted the best for you personally but also for the team. That sort of backing was massive for me and I appreciate it to this day. As a manager Kenny was brilliant for me. He put me in the team, gave me the time and the environment in which to develop, and provided me with the kind of guidance that only someone of his experience could. I even have a constant reminder of what he did for me in the form of the League Cup winner's medal that I won against Cardiff City in 2012. Speak to the other lads who signed for him and they'll say exactly the same."

Dalglish was an old head who Henderson learned lots from. In his first spell as Liverpool boss Dalglish had been in charge when Jordan was born. As Hendo came to Anfield Dalglish was a figure with the stature that was perfect for guiding an ambitious and dedicated player aiming for the top.

Dalglish wasn't the only manager to be impressed by Jordan. Kenny's predecessor Roy Hodgson called Hendo up for England at the end of the season. Already capped once before he came to Liverpool, Henderson would win four more caps before playing for Liverpool again, two of them in the Euro 2020 finals.

As Jordan returned to Melwood for pre-season training the big question would be could he impress the next Liverpool manager in his story? That would be the man who had overseen Dalglish's defeat in his final fixture at Swansea... Brendan Rodgers.

## CHAPTER EIGHT

# DEATH BY FOOTBALL

The day after Brendan Rodgers took over as Liverpool manager Jordan Henderson came off the bench to replace Steven Gerrard as England beat Belgium at Wembley. Evidently Henderson was not going to replace Gerrard in Rodgers' mind, or perhaps even play alongside the Liverpool legend. It is normal practice for managers coming into clubs to want to put their own stamp on their new team. That inevitably means changes in personnel and Rodgers who had seen Liverpool - with Henderson - lose tamely to his Swansea side in their last match before his arrival evidently had his own vision of the way forward. That vision did not necessarily include Hendo who presumably failed to warrant much of a mention in the 180 page dossier Rodgers was said to have prepared for his interview, outlining his vision for Liverpool's future under him.

Having been the first choice of Fenway Sports Group to replace Dalglish, Rodgers breezed into Anfield full of a self-belief bolstered by the understanding that Liverpool had been willing to pay compensation in the region of £7m to secure his release from Swansea rather than going for their second choice, said to be Roberto Martinez. The Wigan boss had been the Premier League Manager of the Month that April and had been one of Rodgers' predecessors at Swansea. Later to take over on the other side of Stanley Park at Everton, Martinez would become Brendan's managerial adversary in Merseyside derbies.

Rodgers gave frees to Fabiano Aurelio, David Amoo, Stephen Darby, Toni Silva and also on the eve of the season Craig Bellamy. He also accepted a mere £1m for cult hero Dirk Kuyt and rid himself of Maxi Rodriguez and Alberto Aquilani.

Beginning to forge a squad in his own image Rodgers' first signing was Fabio Borini. The Italian was signed from Roma but was a former player of Rodgers in the youth ranks at Chelsea and had done well for Brendan during a loan spell with Swansea. Having invested over £10m on Borini a further £15m was paid to bring in midfielder Joe Allen who he had worked with at Swansea, not a good sign for Henderson.

An advocate of possession based football, Rodgers seemingly didn't see Henderson's lung-bursting style fitting into the short-passing 'Tiki-taka' Spanish style he appeared to have in mind for the connoisseurs of Anfield. Technically gifted players, especially those with pace, looked like being the top targets of the Rodgers' recruitment team.

Owners FSG were reportedly urging their new manager to sign Daniel Sturridge. Aged just 22 he had just scored 13 goals for Chelsea, including one against Liverpool, had Champions League experience and had recently won his second England cap. He was seen as one of the brightest young natural talents in the country. Nonetheless Rodgers apparently wasn't as enthusiastic about what Sturridge could bring to his side and needing a striker as he looked to off-load the expensive Andy Carroll set his sights on Fulham's US international Clint Dempsey.

Dempsey had hit 10 more goals for Fulham the previous season than Sturridge had managed in the more palatial surroundings of West London neighbours Chelsea. Only Robin van Persie, Wayne Rooney and Paul Scholes had come ahead of the American in the recently announced Football Writers' Association Footballer of the Year awards and he had scored against England at the most recent World Cup. Dempsey's technique and application combined with his versatility and willingness to adapt to fluidity in formations made him the forward Rodgers viewed as key to his Liverpool vision.

Unlike the arrival of Joe Allen, the potential purchase of Clint Dempsey might not have threatened Jordan Henderson's future at Anfield until, that is, it became known that Rodgers was proposing to offer Hendo to Fulham in part exchange.

Having left his role as Director of Football at Liverpool shortly before the end of the season Damien Comolli was astonished at the prospect of the club giving up a player he had been prepared to have his knuckles rapped for going over-budget on, "I think I called his agent and said, 'What the hell are they doing here? I was laughing at what I was hearing, that they were trying to sell him" he told ESPN, "I thought this is another Gareth Bale, when Harry Redknapp tried to sell him to Nottingham Forest." Redknapp had agreed to sell Bale to Forest's new manager Billy Davies in 2009 only for Bale to do a U-turn and decide to stay at Spurs and fight for his place.

Similarly Henderson had no intention of giving up on his ambition of success with

Liverpool. Reflecting on this episode in years to come on Talksport Henderson admitted, "That was a crucial period in my career. Not only my career but my career in general. I thought that moment was big, and it was a tough moment, but one that I feel helped me, looking back now. I don't know what would have happened if I didn't have that moment. It was tough at the time but thankfully it worked out okay in the end."

With Henderson on England duty during the club close season as Rodgers was installed at Anfield, the manager spoke about how he saw his Liverpool team playing as he looked for a transformation in style leading to ultimate success. Liverpool had just finished a monstrous 27 points behind both of the Manchester clubs, 18 behind Arsenal and even four behind seventh placed Everton. It was to be a long and winding road to the top. "We might not be ready for the title now but the process begins today" outlined the former Swansea supremo who talked of making opponents suffer 'death by football' and provided an insight into his methods and thinking via a six part documentary series, 'Being Liverpool,' which tracked the club's pre-season build up.

Managed by former England centre-forward Paul Mariner, Toronto were the first side to take on a Liverpool team setting out on the Brendan voyage. Appropriately enough the first game under the new boss took place at the Rogers Centre where England youth international Adam Morgan came off the bench to claim Liverpool's equaliser in a 1-1 draw after Quincy Amarikwa had put the Canadians ahead. Rodgers gave 23 players game time, but having been given extra time to rest following Euro 2012, where he had played under a month before Liverpool took on Toronto, Hendo was not part of Rodgers' first viewing of his new squad.

From there it was on 550 miles east to the home of the club's owners at Fenway Park in Boston where Roma were the next in danger of death by football only for Borini's old boys to beat Rodgers' men 2-1 before the club's first trip to the States since 2004 ended with a goalless draw with Tottenham Hotspur in Baltimore. This match, in near 100 degrees fahrenheit heat at the home of NFL side Baltimore Ravens, was Rodgers' first look at Henderson in his side, Jordan coming off the bench to replace Charlie Adam at half-time as Liverpool lined up in a 4-1-2-3 shape.

Competitive action got going before Liverpool completed their pre-season

Jordan celebrates after the 2-1 victory against Wolves at Molineux, 23/01/20

Jordan Henderson celebrates scoring
Sunderland's fourth v Wigan Athletic
at Stadium of Light, 23/04/11

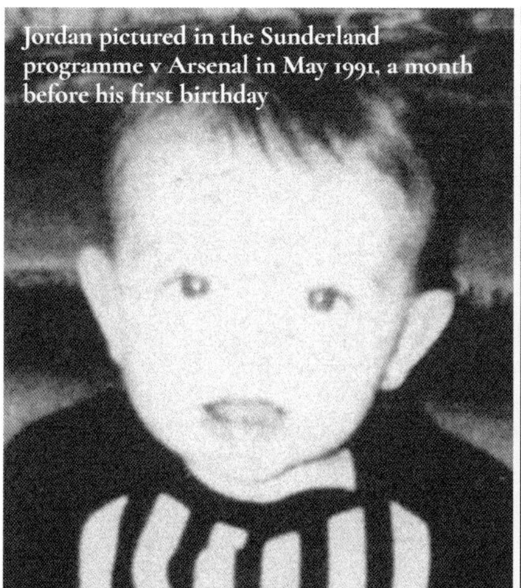
Jordan pictured in the Sunderland programme v Arsenal in May 1991, a month before his first birthday

Jordan with Josh Home-Jackson on the day of their Under 18 debuts in April 2006

Jordan's late winning goal v Charlton Athletic at the Valley in the FA Youth Cup quarter-final, 27/02/08

FA Youth Cup semi-final at Manchester City, 11/03/08

Jordan scores for Coventry City at Norwich, 28/02/09

Jordan in
Sky Blue action on
his Coventry debut
at Derby on 31/01/09

Jordan in action against Yann M'Vila on his England debut v France at Wembley, 17/11/10

Liverpool Press Conference shortly after signing for the Reds, 03/08/11

Jordan scores his first Liverpool goal v Bolton Wanderers at Anfield, 27/08/11

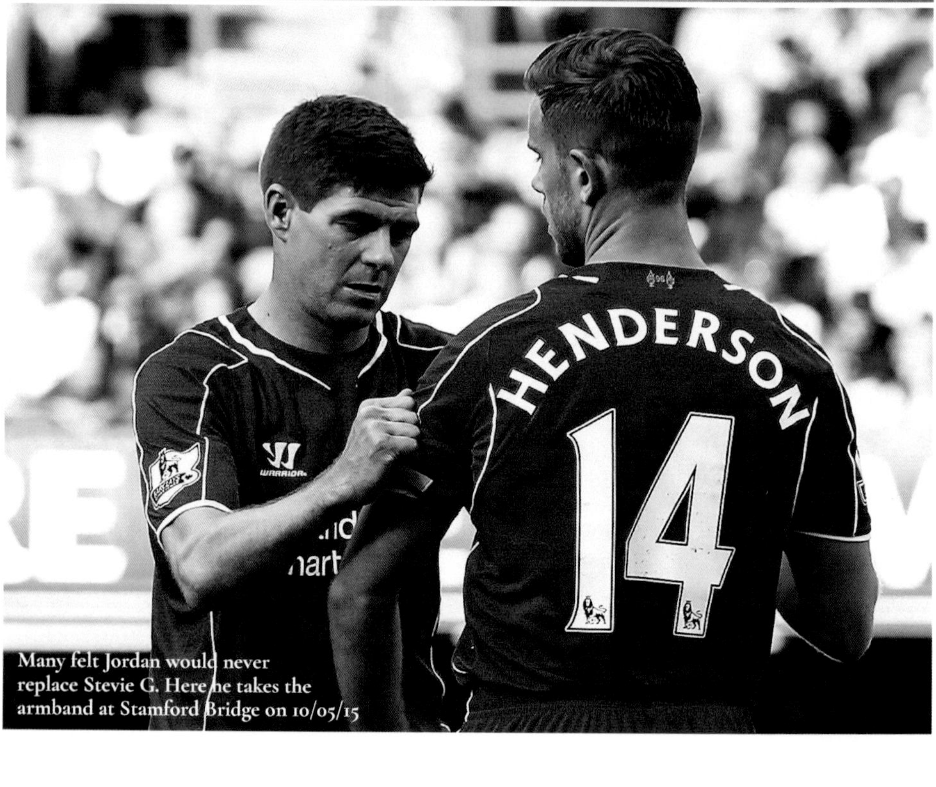

Many felt Jordan would never replace Stevie G. Here he takes the armband at Stamford Bridge on 10/05/15

Jordan in England action during the 2018 FIFA World Cup semi-final match against Croatia, 11/07/18

Liverpool's Champions League victory parade, 02/06/19

All smiles with Jurgen Klopp after the Club World Cup semi-final v Monterrey, 18/12/19

friendlies. Starting in Belarus against Gomel Rodgers named Henderson in his first competitive Liverpool side but saw Stewart Downing be the player to impress as the winger looked for a fresh start, scoring the only goal of the game two minutes after Henderson had been replaced by Lucas Leiva.

A week later Liverpool won the return leg easily with Borini capping an impressive home debut with a goal in a 3-0 win. Jordan was left on the bench, Jay Spearing getting the nod ahead of him when Rodgers decided to allow the much loved Lucas a round of applause with a late substitution. As Hendo kicked his heels, desperate to play there was more bad news for him as watching from the directors' box was Joe Allen, about to be signed by Rodgers as he looked to increase his team's ability to pass opponents to death.

48 hours later Lucas scored in the first half as Rodgers' dress rehearsal for the Premier League kick-off brought Sami Hyppia's Bayer Leverkusen to Anfield for a friendly, on a day when 17-year old Raheem Sterling scored in just the third minute of his first Anfield start. With Allen in the stands again Henderson got an opportunity to come on at the interval but with the second half drawn 1-1 in contrast to the 2-0 half time lead the signs were not great for Hendo as he looked to fight for his future.

The opening day of Brendan Rodgers' first Premier League season with Liverpool took the Reds to West Bromwich Albion. The Baggies also had a new manager in situ. Kenny Dalglish's former coach Steve Clarke had taken over at the Hawthorns where a vacancy had arisen due to Liverpool failure Roy Hodgson getting the England job.

As the season kicked off in the sunshine the new look Liverpool lined up with Lucas, Allen and Gerrard in the middle of the park with Downing, Suarez and Borini up front. Jordan was on the bench where Liverpool's strength in depth was illustrated by the fact that if Rodgers were to look over his shoulder wondering about a midfielder to introduce he had a choice of Joe Cole, Charlie Adam and Jonjo Shelvey as well as Henderson.

Liverpool's aim to keep the ball and pass their opponents off the park worked reasonably well early on as the Reds moved the ball around but with Albion's defence not pulled out of position. If the aim was to wear the Baggies down and strike as they tired that target took a hit just before half time when Rodgers' team talk needed to be re-adjusted as Zoltan Gera celebrated his return from a cruciate ligament injury by blasting the opener.

Things went from bad to worse just shy of the hour mark when Daniel Agger was sent off in conceding a penalty and though Pepe Reina kept Liverpool in the game by saving Sean Long's spot kick it was a mere six minute reprise as Peter Odemwingie made no mistake with a second penalty given away by Martin Skrtel. Having sacrificed Downing for Jamie Carragher due to the sending off, Rodgers replaced Lucas with the more attack minded Cole in response to going two down. When Cole then hurt his hamstring Hendo, Adam and Shelvey were snubbed as the man who aimed for death by football decided to go route one with the introduction of Andy Carroll. The game had already been killed when Chelsea loanee Romelu Lukaku headed home a Liam Ridgewell cross to make it 3-0 with 13 minutes left.

As the unused subs headed for the coach they will have known the performance at least improved their chances of involvement, while if Rodgers felt Rome wasn't built in a day there were critics ready to tell him Rome didn't cost as much to build as his line-up.

The trio of unused midfielders all got a chance to start in Liverpool's next game, as did Jay Spearing. The occasion was a Europa League game in Edinburgh at Hearts where a late own goal gave Liverpool a narrow first leg lead. Things might have been much better had Borini not fluffed a first half chance laid on a plate for him by a glorious pass from Henderson.

The end of the transfer window approached with ongoing speculation concerning Liverpool's interest in Fulham's Clint Dempsey, and therefore Henderson's potential use as a make-weight. Rodgers reverted to the same midfield he had used at West Brom for the weekend visit of Manchester City, but when Lucas pulled up with an injury in only the fifth minute it was Shelvey who was chosen to come on. Again Henderson was left kicking his heels with the possibility that the match at Hearts might have been his last game for the club.

That could have continued to be the case as 24 hours before the window closed Jordan again played against Hearts but was brought off with quarter of an hour to go as Liverpool struggled to break down the Scots. A late Suarez goal squeezed Rodgers' men through after a 1-1 draw on the night but having also drawn with Man City following the loss at the Hawthorns this was not the beginning anyone at Anfield was looking for.

That dismal start continued as Arsenal – who were yet to score in the season as they entered Anfield – breezed to a 2-0 win. With Southampton pointless after three games, Liverpool joined QPR, Aston Villa and Reading on one point. It was the club's worst league start in half a century but still Henderson was yet to play a single minute in the Premier League, again being left as an unused sub.

By now he had yet more competition for a shirt, Rodgers having acquired Turkey international Nuri Sahin on a season long loan from Real Madrid. Sahin had gone straight into the starting line-up against the Gunners and when withdrawn two thirds of the way through the match once again it was Shelvey who was the preferred option off the bench.

While Liverpool had recruited Sahin and also secured Moroccan forward Oussama Assaidi from Dutch club Heerenveen for £2.4m, as well as German teenage striker Samed Yesil for £1m from Bayer Leverkusen, they had not secured the signature of the much talked about Clint Dempsey. He had moved across London to Tottenham on transfer deadline day for the value for money fee of £6m – a sixth of the price Liverpool had paid for Andy Carroll who Rodgers had let go on loan to West Ham. All Liverpool had in the meantime was to face the prospect of trouble from the Premier League having been reported by Fulham for tapping up Dempsey.

As Rodgers spoke about Liverpool's players getting used to his possession based system it was evident they had a long way to go. While two goals to nil was the statistic that counted against Arsenal the underlying figure of passes from the relevant midfield trios told a sorry tale for a team who wanted to keep the ball. Arsenal's midfield totalled 228 passes to Liverpool's 157.

Henderson was not just out of the Liverpool team at this time. Having been part of the England squad at the summer's Euro's he could not even get into Roy Hodgson's squad for World Cup qualifying games away to Moldova and at home to Ukraine. Instead he was selected for the Under 21 squad, playing in 2-0 and 1-0 victories away to Azerbaijan – where Shelvey scored – and at home to Norway in Chesterfield.

So it was that having left his boyhood club Sunderland to move to Liverpool with big ambitions, that after winning the Young Player of the Year award in his first year at Anfield, following the international break he returned to the Stadium of Light still not able to get into the Liverpool side. This time as Jordan once again remained an unused sub, Shelvey was promoted into the starting line-up with newcomer Sahin sat alongside Hendo as Luis Suarez's late goal rescued a point for Liverpool in yet another draw.

It was an emotional time at the club, the game at Sunderland being the first since the Hillsborough Independent Panel ruled that no Liverpool supporters were in any way responsible for the disaster on that awful day in 1989, a time before Jordan Henderson was born but a time and a date that will stay forever imprinted in the minds of every football supporter, whether Liverpool is their club or not. The persistence and sheer love and desire for justice of the Hillsborough Family Support Group had had a great victory even if fans were still waiting for any victory in the Premier League under Rodgers.

Victory did come with Henderson in the side for the full 90 minutes in the next game as five were scored away from home to Young Boys in the Europa League. Jordan's cause was not especially helped however as three goals were conceded to a moderate side. Rodgers had left his big hitters at home and included three debutants including two teenagers in a largely second string line-up while Jonjo Shelvey rubber stamped his place in the manager's thoughts by coming off the bench and scoring a couple of well-taken goals.

Three days later Shelvey let Rodgers down when being sent off shortly before half time in an Anfield showdown with Manchester United. The game was preceded by moving commemorations in the first home fixture since the publication of the Hillsborough findings. In a typically pulsating clash with United Steven Gerrard gave 10 man Liverpool the lead. With Sir Alex Ferguson's team quickly equalising the game was on a knife edge when Rodgers finally decided to give Hendo his first Premier League appearance under him, swapping him for Raheem Sterling with 66 minutes gone. Jordan was swiftly into the action, offering his energy and industry to a side still trying to cope a player short but ultimately it was to no avail as a late van Persie penalty took the points to Manchester.

With Everton third on 10 points from five games the table didn't make for glorious reading for Liverpool fans. Rodgers' team were third bottom, level on two points with second bottom QPR and a point ahead of back markers Reading who had a game in hand. It was the first time since 1911 Liverpool had failed to win one of their first five league games. Back then Liverpool were also third bottom with two points after a defeat to West Bromwich Albion and it was Albion who were next up with a quick return to the Hawthorns, this time in the Capital One (League) Cup.

Once again Hendo was selected for the cup team, but with seven teenagers involved, including 16-year old sub Jerome Sinclair who became the club's youngest ever player, it was evident that Jordan remained part of the second string in the eyes of the Gaffer. Nonetheless he played his part in a 2-1 victory which contrasted sharply with the opening day Premier League loss at the same venue.

At this point Henderson was just starting to come into Rodgers' mind as more than a cup player. Having come off the bench in the previous Premier League game he was introduced at exactly the same moment two thirds of the way through the next one. Despite their awful start Liverpool had already won four away games in cup competitions. On this occasion at Norwich they won spectacularly, a Suarez hat-trick being the highlight of a 5-2 victory in which the Uruguayan had already laid claim to the match ball before Henderson was introduced with the score 4-1.

While Jordan was now playing bit parts in league games and regularly starting cup matches he was still a player Brendan Rodgers evidently looked upon as dispensable, a squad player at best. The next four games were at home. In these he was subbed in a Europa League defeat at the hands of Udinese, played a total of five minutes in a couple of Premier League games in which Liverpool scored once and was left on the bench for a narrow Europa League win over Anzhi Makhachkala. Very much on the fringes at Anfield he continued to also be absent from the England squad, not selected for that month's internationals with San Marino and Poland.

Remaining part of Stuart Pearce's England Under 21 set-up continued to provide Jordan with competitive football in a team where he was a main man. The October international break saw him play both 90 minutes as hard-fought 1-0 wins over Serbia were achieved at Norwich and in the Mladost Stadium in Krusevac in key

Under 21 Championship preliminaries play-offs.

Following a late cameo in a derby draw at Everton he started cup defeats at home to Rodgers' former club Swansea and the return with Anzhi in Russia either side of watching a home draw with Newcastle from the sub's bench. After another idle 90 minutes as an unused sub at Chelsea things started to look up. Brought on as first half sub in a comfortable home win over Wigan there was a start in the home game with Young Boys before a first Premier League start under Rodgers. It came at the same place as Jordan's last Premier start, at the Gaffer's old club Swansea where Rodgers was able to emerge with pride intact after a goalless draw, albeit slowly improving Liverpool were still beneath Michael Laudrup's Swans in the table.

Hendo had done enough to keep his place but was the first man brought off in the following defeat at Spurs. Back on the bench for the next game, a narrow home win against Southampton Jordan again had a taste of the action before boarding the plane for a key game in Italy.

The final Group game with Udinese was one Liverpool had to win to be sure of staying in Europe. Win they did with Hendo's first European goal and Jordan also going close to scoring a second. In a match where he supplied a steady stream of good balls to the ever dangerous Suarez Henderson scored the only goal of the match, firing a low shot through the legs of Daniele Padelli although the keeper later denied him with a superlative save from an excellently executed volley. With a three way tie at the top of the table with Liverpool, Anzhi and Young Boys all on ten points, Liverpool topped it on goals scored with Young Boys missing out by a single goal.

Having scored the key goal that ensured the club's qualification for the knock-out stage of the Europa League Hendo had made a notable contribution in addition to the tireless and unselfish work he routinely did for the team. With another transfer window fewer than four weeks away he was giving the manager reason to reconsider his willingness to trade him.

Nonetheless there was a long way to go. The next four games saw Jordan on the bench, failing to get on in one of them, ironically a big home win against a Fulham team he could have been returning to Anfield with. On the eve of the transfer window he did start in West London, helping Liverpool to a 3-0 win at QPR, playing for over an hour despite being ill although Rodgers was ill himself and didn't see the match which was overseen by his assistant Colin Pascoe. Nonetheless the performance reiterated Hendo's reliability and determination. Three days later Henderson started again in another 3-0 win, against his old club Sunderland, this time witnessed by the Gaffer who already had a new addition to his squad, having finally brought in Daniel Sturridge.

Liverpool managing director Ian Ayre spoke of the signing, saying, "Daniel is somebody we've always had in our sights and somebody the manager has had huge interest in right from the start. I'm very pleased that we've got the right player and the right deal." Rumoured to be in the region of £12m the actual cost of the right deal was shrouded in mystery as the transfer fee from Chelsea remained undisclosed while how keen Rodgers was on a player he apparently could have had in the summer was subject to some speculation. Sturridge had missed much of the first half of the season due to a hamstring injury which meant it was over six weeks since he had kicked a ball in anger when he arrived at Anfield.

Any doubts Rodgers might have secretly harboured about a player his employers seemed keener on than him – at least initially – must have been largely dispelled quickly as after scoring in each of his first three games a goal in a 5-0 trouncing of Brendan's old boys Swansea gave Sturridge five goals in his first seven appearances.

Sturridge was far from Liverpool's solitary January investment. A fee of £8.5m would prove a bargain for the acquisition of Inter and Brazil midfielder Philippe Coutinho. Although Joe Cole had been allowed to leave on a free to West Ham the arrival of another top class player in Coutinho could only make the competition for a midfield place ever tougher for Henderson. Despite the number of appearances he had made the previous year, and regardless of his Young Player of the Year award and Euro 2012 experience Jordan was still only barely flickering on Rodgers' radar.

At Liverpool the bar is constantly raised. Coutinho's arrival came just as Jordan had got into the groove. Although not helped by being part of the team knocked out of the FA Cup by Oldham, having previously only once started back to back Premier League games under the manager he was seeking to convince of his worth he started four successive Premier games and scored in two of them.

However Steve Clarke's return to Merseyside coincided with a night when Hendo was hooked after an hour and Countinho later came on for his debut. Goalless when Jordan came off, Liverpool suffered a 2-0 home defeat by the Baggies after Steve G failed with a penalty with the score-line still blank. Henderson kept his place for a trip to Zenit St. Petersburg three days later but after another disappointing 2-0 loss arrived at Anfield for the following clash with Swansea and found himself back on the bench as Coutinho lined up for a full debut.

Determined as ever to rise to the occasion it was as Philippe Coutinho arrived that Jordan pushed on and forced himself into the Liverpool line-up regardless of the quality of competition. Having come on to replace Coutinho on the Brazilian's full debut Hendo started the next match in the Europa League (as Liverpool bowed out of Europe on away goals despite beating Zenit 3-1) and then after three consecutive substitute outings in the Premier League – two of them late cameos – got a start and a goal in a good win at Aston Villa .

Staying in the team for the next three games he then returned to his native north east for a fixture at Newcastle. This was the place where after being jeered for a fluffed free kick he had undertaken such extra individual practise it had been the story that persuaded Damien Comolli to break his budget to bring Hendo to Liverpool.

Newcastle fans found that Hendo had indeed been practising his free kicks as after their French full-back Mathieu Debuchy was sent off for a clumsy foul on Coutinho Henderson curled home Liverpool's sixth and his own second goal of the game. The home side were embarrassed as in the 51st game under Brendan Rodgers Liverpool did indeed inflict death by football on their opponents. Liverpool were irresistible as in the style of the very best sides team play completely overtook individual greed.

At 1-0 Sturridge had a great chance to score but laid the ball on a plate for the onrushing Henderson to have a tap in as his chance was greater. Later the compliment was returned as Hendo eschewed a shooting opportunity to roll the ball in front of Sturridge who had an empty goal to shoot into, something he did before adapting his trademark slinky dance celebration to point to Hendo who had laid the goal on. Both players came off with two goals and an assist to their name. The performance had been so good as they inflicted Newcastle's biggest home defeat since 1925 that no-one seemed to notice Liverpool had been missing Luis Suarez. The Uruguayan had been suspended for having an early taste of Champions League success after taking a chunk out of Chelsea's Branislav Ivanovic the previous weekend.

Champions League success at this point was still a long way off for Liverpool but Henderson had proved to the manager who started the season wanting to sell him that he deserved to earn a place at Liverpool. Despite being on the fringe of the team for so much of the season, come the end of the campaign only Steven Gerrard and Stewart Downing had appeared in more games than the 44 Henderson had managed to play some part of.

"At the start, it wasn't working out how I'd planned. I wasn't playing much and found it difficult to get into the team" reflected Jordan later. Just as he would in due course not take umbrage at Sir Alex Ferguson's unkind comments about his running style, Henderson had never grumbled about being left out of Rodgers' team. Unusually for anyone in any walk of life, let alone footballers, instead of looking for someone to blame when things weren't going well Jordan had looked at himself and how he could improve. It is a trait that has been consistent throughout his career. "I always still had a good relationship with the manager and I felt as though I could definitely improve under him, even though I wasn't playing as much as I would have liked" he told Talksport, adding, "We had conversations on what I needed to improve on to get into the team, and I had a good feeling that I could definitely do that. I wanted to stay, improve under Brendan Rodgers, show him that I could get into the team and stay there, and I could have a big part to play."

Still only 22 when Liverpool's season ended, Jordan was still developing. For the fourth year in a row he picked up a Young Player of the Year award, this time for England Under 21s. Having played for the senior squad in the Euro's the previous summer, some players might have seen it as a step down to be back in the Under 21s. In typical fashion Henderson viewed it as an opportunity.

After playing Under 21 football in the early season friendlies and the double-header showdown with Serbia Henderson had started comfortable home friendly victories over Northern Ireland, Sweden and Romania as well as coming off the bench to replace Raheem Sterling in a 4-0 win over an Austria side who had two men sent off at Brighton.

Still not getting much of a rest after playing in the senior Euros the previous summer Henderson headed off to the UEFA Under 21 Championship finals in Israel. That rest before the start of his third season with Liverpool would come quicker than anticipated after England had a disastrous tournament.

After going into the finals on the back of a nine game winning streak in which they hadn't conceded, England lost all three group games and were on the first plane back home. Having seen Napoli hot-shot Lorenzo Insigne score with a 79th minute free kick in the opening match with Italy, captain Henderson went agonisingly close to a last minute equaliser of his own, only to see keeper Francesco Bardi just keep his set-piece out.

Jordan went close to scoring in the second game too but a left-footed shot that brought a flying save out of Orjan Nyland Haskjold and a header that went just wide could not disguise a poor display by England who were well beaten 3-1 by Norway. With England already out and hosts Israel all but mathematically out the final group game was a dead rubber in which Jordan came on for Tom Ince at half time only to see Israel complete England's pointless record when Ofir Krieff scored a late winner on his home ground in Jerusalem.

Thirty two days after wrapping up his 2012-13 campaign in the Promised Land, Hendo was back in a Liverpool shirt, playing at Preston in the Shankly Shield, the opening friendly of the new campaign. Promisingly, he was in the starting line-up, not that anything can be read from early pre-season line-ups but at least it was a good omen for a player who had turned 23 during his month off.

Including loans Liverpool brought in eight new faces by the time that summer's transfer window ended, but none of them would be in direct competition with Hendo other than perhaps Luis Alberto, a near £7m buy from Seville. However with Jonjo Shelvey, Jay Spearing and an assortment of fringe midfielders moving out competition for places in the Anfield engine room would be fewer in number if not in quality. The calibre of the squad would continue to include Luis Suarez despite a summer of speculation that he would join Arsenal, albeit Suarez started the season still suspended owing to his appetite for biting Chelsea's Ivanovic.

A globe-trotting pre-season took in games in Indonesia, Australia, Thailand, Norway and Ireland as well as Stevie G's Testimonial against Olympiacos where Henderson scored with a sublime chip with his first touch after coming on as a sub.

The real stuff got started with a narrow opening day win over Stoke at Anfield, debutant goalkeeper Simon Mignolet ensuring the win bonus with a late penalty save. The keeper's heroics might not have been needed if the woodwork had not thwarted Henderson earlier but Jordan did have an excellent assist to his name for the only goal of the game scored by Daniel Sturridge.

Compared to Rodgers' first season there was by now an important change for Jordan. Whereas when Rodgers arrived Henderson seemed to be surplus to requirements, now he was very much part of the manager's plans. Regardless of the top quality around him in the Liverpool midfield Hendo was there on merit. Moreover, now increasingly established in L4, after a first season as a young player under Dalglish when he had to cope with more than his fair share of doubters and a second season where the doubters included his new manager, Henderson's re-establishment as a regular first teamer coincided with the rise of the Reds.

Eighth and seventh in his first two seasons, Liverpool would achieve 84 points and score 101 Premier League goals as they ran Chelsea close for the title. The league goals tally was something the club had not managed since 1895-96! Henderson would start every Premier game until crucially missing three of the last four after marking his 101st league appearance for the club with an uncharacteristic straight red card in a win over Manchester City for a rash challenge on Samir Nasri.

Beating City left Liverpool top of the table. With four games left Brendan's boys were two points clear of Chelsea and while Manchester City had two games in hand their defeat at Anfield left them seven points adrift. Surely this would be Liverpool's time to finally win the Premier League. With games to come against Norwich followed by a potential title decider with Chelsea at Anfield, followed by less than daunting fixtures with Palace and Newcastle, Liverpool were favourites.

Hendo's old Sunderland club appeared to have done Liverpool a favour when the bottom of the league team won at Chelsea 24 hours before Liverpool won at Carrow Road to open up a five point gap with three games to go.

Next time out Chelsea had to come to Anfield in the knowledge that defeat would eliminate them from the title race. Liverpool had managed without Henderson at Norwich but he was sorely missed in what proved to be a crucial 2-0 home defeat to the Mourinho masterminded Blues. Rodgers moaned Chelsea had parked two buses not one but ultimately they had a ticket to ride, not least after Stevie G slipped to present Demba Ba with a clear run on goal to break the deadlock.

Worse was to come as Henderson sat out the final match of his three game ban as Liverpool went to Crystal Palace. Coming back from 3-0 down had provided one of the club's greatest nights in Istanbul in the Champions League final against Milan under a decade earlier but at what became known as Crystanbul this time Liverpool tossed away a three goal lead to drop two points that cost them the Premier League title the club craved. Astonishingly only 11 minutes were left when Liverpool imploded.

Defeat by Chelsea had handed the initiative to Manchester City who were on course to take the title on goal difference – as they had when pipping local rivals United with the 'Aguerooo!' moment two years earlier – if both they and Liverpool won their remaining games. Pressure told when out of the blue Damien Delaney pulled one back for Palace in the 79th minute and then substitute Dwight Gayle bagged a late double to earn the Eagles a point but leave the Liver Bird crestfallen. Distraught, ashen faced fans and players departed Selhurst Park with their title dreams in tatters.

Henderson was back for the final match where victory over Newcastle gave Liverpool 80 points from the 35 games he had started but their inability to collect more than a paltry four points from the three games he missed left them trailing champions City by two points.

It was a barren year in cup competitions too. Unlike the double Wembley finals of Hendo's initial year under Dalgish, Liverpool had progressed through just two and one rounds of the domestic cup competitions before elimination at the hands of Arsenal and Manchester United while not having qualified for Europe they had been able to focus on their title charge.

Nonetheless Jordan did get to Wembley for the Capital One Cup final, turning up in a black hoodie with the hood up to try and escape recognition as he sat amongst the Sunderland fans as his home town team took on Manchester City who took that trophy as well as the title.

Attending as a fan was not Henderson's first visit of the season to the national stadium. His return as a regular at his club had brought about a return to the senior international fold with four Wembley appearances during the campaign, three of them before his appearance in the stands. Hodgson had recalled him for November friendlies with Chile and Germany, both of which were lost as he came off the bench.

With the World Cup in Brazil approaching it was a good time to return to the squad.

There were also late season starts in wins over Denmark and Peru before once again Jordan's summer was taken up with international football. Given 90 minutes split over two warm up games in Miami Hendo was one of five Liverpool players in the starting line-up for the first game of the World Cup against Italy. Although club-mate Sturridge scored, so did his forthcoming Anfield colleague Mario Balotelli as England got off to a losing start.

Five days later it was another familiar face who destroyed English hopes, Suarez's brace bringing defeat to Uruguay with Henderson substituted as he had been in the first game. With England already out Henderson sat out the final dead rubber draw with Costa Rica as a season that had promised so much for club and country again ended in anti-climax. With Brendan Rodgers having been named as the Manager of the Season and signing a new contract at Anfield Henderson by now was an increasingly important member of the Liverpool set-up. Gone were the days of him not being part of the manager's plans and most supporters now appreciated what he brought to the team, even if there have always been some who are oblivious to the unselfish work he does off the ball and remain critical. Liverpool fans like to be thought of as amongst the most knowledgeable in the game but that minority do their reputation no favours.

Having got so close to the title everyone with Liverpool at heart had serious ambitions of going one better in the coming 2014-15 season. It was evident that Rodgers needed to tighten a leaky defence that had conceded 50 goals – almost 25% more than champions City - but attack wise it was surely a case of same again please. That hope was wrecked when Suarez got his longed for move to Barcelona for a club record £75m.

Over £40m more was spent than was received for Suarez as Liverpool splashed the cash. Southampton pocketed close to £50m for the transfers of Adam Lallana. Rickie Lambert and Dejan Lovren while Emre Can arrived from Bayer Leverkusen, Lazar Markovic from Benfica, Divock Origi from Lille and Spanish full-backs Alberto Moreno and Javier Manquillo arrived from Seville and Atletico Madrid, Manquillo initially on loan. With the transfer window into its last week the talented but troublesome Milan forward Mario Balotelli was also added to the squad at a cost of £16m.

Amongst the players joining Suarez through the exit door was Daniel Agger just before the window closed, a move that meant Liverpool needed a new vice-captain. "Jordan is someone who represents the best values of what we are all about, as a team and as a club" declared Brendan Rodgers in announcing Henderson as Liverpool's new vice-captain to Steven Gerrard. He continued, "Jordan is completely dedicated to the game and his leadership qualities come from the example he sets. It's another great story for Jordan in his journey as a Liverpool player and it shows the great progress he has made."

Given a delayed start following his World Cup trip, Henderson hadn't been involved in the opening couple of friendlies, getting his first run out in a late sub in a 1-0 defeat to Roma at Fenway Park in Boston. He was then straight into the thick of it playing the full game as Olympiacos were beaten by an early Raheem Sterling goal as the Guinness Champions Cup got going at Soldier Field in Chicago. The same competition then saw Hendo score and add another in a penalty shoot-out as Manchester City were beaten at the Yankee Stadium before he also appeared in a win over AC Milan and a 3-1 defeat to Manchester United in the final. Finally, in his first match back in England since before the World Cup he scored in a dress rehearsal for the season as Borussia Dortmund were defeated 4-0 at Anfield.

Bill Shankly once noted that, "Football is like a piano. You need eight men to carry it and three who can play the damn thing." In 2013-14 Jordan had been one of those carrying the piano, doing vast amounts of running while Stevie G operated in a deep role pulling the strings. More was to be expected of Henderson in 2014-15. While always a man who puts the team first, you don't get to play regularly for Liverpool by being no more than a piano carrier, regardless of the wit and wisdom of Shanks.

Bending a brilliant pass from inside his own half to release Sterling to score on the opening day of the season illustrated Hendo's ability to tinkle the ivories in a footballing sense. The fact that this superb assist against Southampton was made with his left foot was noted by keener students of what the player had to offer.

It was a bright start to the season and one which shone even brighter in the coming weeks. Outstanding in wins over Spurs and Ludogorets of Bulgaria in his first Champions League game, Hendo maintained a passing accuracy close to 90% in his opening 10 games during which he added another couple of assists and the winner in a home win over West Brom. With Rodgers showing his usual fluidity of formation Jordan's consistency came regardless of his versatility either playing wide in a midfield diamond, operating in a deep lying role or pushing on in support of his forwards. Whichever part of the piano he was asked to hold or play Hendo was reliable as part of the road crew or as a virtuoso.

Maintaining his value to the national side, adding five more caps by mid-November, there was another landmark in the Jordan Henderson story three days after he scored his first Champions League goal in a draw at Ludogorets, where one of his sprints from inside his own half paid off as he arrived with immaculate timing to finish off a low Sterling centre. For over half the game Hendo's goal looked like being a winner only for a late leveller by Georgi Terziev to continue a disappointing run of results for the Anfielders. Liverpool had lost their previous four games with their only victory in the last seven coming in a Capital One Cup tie at home to Swansea where they had been saved by two goals after the 86th minute.

Having hoped to go one better than their runners up spot of the year before Rodgers' Reds found themselves in the bottom half of the table ahead of the visit of Stoke City. It wasn't a good time as in addition to naming almost £90m worth of summer signings as substitutes, on what was the 16th anniversary of Steven Gerrard's first team debut Rodgers left him on the bench, insisting he was giving his 34-year old captain a breather as the Christmas period approached. With the Liverpool captain's armband proudly sported by Jordan for the first time the game was a struggle, Henderson going as close as anyone to scoring before Glen Johnson came to the rescue five minutes from time with his first goal since 2012 as a 1-0 win was squeaked. Ten minutes earlier Stevie G had come on for Lucas, the match programme having heavily featured the skipper's anniversary but as the teams trooped off Hendo had a winning start as skipper under his belt.

Despite the return of the winning feeling which continued next time out as both restored skipper Stevie G and future captain Henderson scored in a win at 10 man Leicester this wasn't a good spell for Jordan or the team. Held to home draws by Sunderland and Basle, the latter occasion saw Liverpool's Champions League return end with demotion to the Europa League. This was followed by a 3-0 rout by Manchester United at Old Trafford which left Jordan and co 10th, eleven days before Christmas, a huge 18 points behind leaders Chelsea and seven points adrift of the consolation prize of fourth.

By this stage Rodgers had largely reverted to a 4-2-3-1 shape with Henderson and Gerrard patrolling in front of the back four and Jordan's role primarily being one of mainly carrying rather than playing Shanks' piano. Needing to change to rekindle the sparkle of the previous season, even without Suarez, the manager found a new system that evolved into Lucas taking responsibility for shielding the defence. Emre Can operated as the right-sided centre-back in a back three with the Spanish duo of Manquillo and Moreno flanking Lucas and Hendo in support of a mobile front three of Sterling, Coutinho and Adam Lallana with Sterling in the lead strike role.

The turn of the year saw Liverpool score four for the first time all season, Jordan getting the assist for Alberto Moreno's opening goal on a day when Swansea's Jonjo Shelvey returned to Anfield to score – albeit through his own goal.

After the pre-Christmas beating at Manchester United Liverpool would not lose again until the end of February when they went out of Europe on penalties at Besiktas on a night neither Hendo or Gerrard were involved. Gerrard was certainly involved the next time Liverpool lost – being sent off just 38 seconds after coming on as a half-time sub in the return fixture with Manchester United after appearing to stamp on Juan Mata, leaving the experienced referee Martin Atkinson little option but to dismiss him. Gerrard had taken the armband from Hendo but had to hand it back as he left his side a man down, albeit to Liverpool's credit they lost only by the odd goal in three. It was a costly defeat as having climbed to fifth during their revival victory would have taken Liverpool into the top four above fourth placed United.

A month to the day after signing off the previous season with England Jordan was stepping out for his first game as Liverpool's full time captain at the Rajamangala National Stadium in Thailand as Liverpool strolled to a 4-0 victory over the Thai All Stars. After playing in a couple of games in Australia, one in Malaysia and another in Finland Jordan sat out the final warm up game at Swindon before the real stuff started.

By a quirk of the fixture list the opening day of the season took Liverpool back to the scene of their recent 6-1 defeat at Stoke. This time, with five debutants, they kept a clean sheet and bagged the points four minutes from time thanks to Phillipe Coutinho.

Leading the side out at Anfield against AFC Bournemouth for the first time since Gerrard's departure Hendo again was part of a 1-0 win but what should have been a great day turned into an awful one. It started well, Jordan supplying the cross that gave Benteke a goal on his home debut. The assist was Henderson's 10th since the start of the previous season – more than any other English player in that period. However having not suffered a notable injury since damaging his ankle in February 2010 when still with Sunderland the new skipper hurt his heel.

It would be the last game he played for Rodgers who was sacked before his new skipper regained fitness having discovered he was suffering from a metatarsal fracture. The team missed Henderson's input, appearing rudderless at times. Having won the first two games under their new captain without conceding a goal Liverpool went 12 games with just one win – unless you count a strong side beating Carlisle United 3-2 on penalties after being held over 120 minutes at Anfield by the League Two minnows, as Liverpool were booed by their own supporters for the second time in four days having suffered the same fate when held by Norwich.

Nine games into that 12 match sequence Rodgers reached the end of the road with his dismissal by FSG coming just an hour after the conclusion of a 1-1 draw at Everton that left Liverpool 10th in the table going into an international break.

Jordan had worn the skipper's armband in just two competitive games under Rodgers since being appointed captain. "It was a huge honour" he acknowledged after the first of those occasions, explaining, "Obviously [Brendan Rodgers] had seen the responsibility and leadership within me and felt I could lead Liverpool and that gave me a lot of confidence. Without Brendan I wouldn't be where I am today."

Henderson played 140 games for Rodgers, probably around 130 more than Rodgers envisaged when he was looking to off-load a young player he initially didn't see as part of his plans. By the time Rodgers left Liverpool he knew what Dalglish had known and Klopp would come to know in addition to the men who managed Hendo at other clubs and internationally, and that is that any team with Jordan Henderson in it is stronger as a unit with him than without him.

## CHAPTER NINE

# JURGEN AND JORDAN

"If anybody who is with us doesn't see the quality of Jordan Henderson, I can't help him. Is Hendo the perfect football player? No. Do I know anybody who is? No. Is he unbelievably important for us? Yes." Jurgen Klopp's summary of his captain is as incisive as a Liverpool counter attack.

Klopp usually looks like he wants to play. To Jurgen the technical area is like a prison cell to an innocent man. When a big goal is scored it looks like the cell door is open as he sprints down the touchline. The final whistle signals the end of his sentence as he can't wait to get onto the pitch, hug his players, salute the crowd, speak to the referee and acknowledge his opponents. For any manager a captain he can trust is imperative, but to a manager like Klopp where the teamwork and discipline within it is not negotiable a skipper who is on the same wavelength as him is essential.

Jurgen and Jordan are kindred spirits. Both are single minded. Neither seem particularly interested in being praised because by the time the latest piece of silverware has been raised they are already thinking about what comes next. Their interest is in how they can improve and how they can help the team to improve. Satisfaction for them is a journey not a destination. Neither ever appears to think 'job done.' Instead they see achievement as an ongoing quest for betterment. Games are just part of the journey, perhaps like roundabouts where the next turning can be a good one or a bad one. Preparation for each part of this trip is the key to success so their focus is not turned on and off, it is there as a constant, wired into their systems.

"Hendo, from my point of view, is a brilliant player. He's our skipper, he's a fantastic character. If I had to write a book about Hendo, it would be 500 pages" said Jurgen in April 2019, evidently with even more to say than this rather shorter book manages to offer. "The most difficult job in the last 500 years of football was to replace Steven Gerrard" Klopp continued. "In the mind of the people it was like if it's not Stevie, then it's not good enough. And he has dealt with that outstandingly well so he can be really proud. Now we have to think of the future and he is a very important part of our team."

Klopp is the ideal manager for Henderson. They share a footballing philosophy where everyone has to give everything. It is reminiscent of Bill Shankly's definition of socialism, "I believe the only way to live and to be truly successful is by collective effort, with everyone working for each other, everyone helping each other, and everyone having a share of the rewards at the end of the day." Klopp's system depends on this. Football's history is littered with sets of great individuals who did not work as a unit and failed to fulfil their potential. Teams of less gifted players achieved much greater success by working together like a colony of ants, achieving much more than they appear capable of because they share the load.

The gegenpressing system Klopp had used to great effect at Borussia Dortmund he imported to Liverpool. "Think about the passes you have to make to get a player in a number 10 role into a position where he can play the genius pass," Klopp once explained. "Gegenpressing lets you win back the ball nearer to the goal. It's only one pass away from a really good opportunity. No playmaker in the world can be as good as a good gegenpressing situation, and that's why it's so important."

For a coach with such a philosophy, a captain with the desire and energy to lead by example and the ability to ensure that everyone on the pitch is constantly urged to contribute, is vital. At Klopp's Liverpool the collective thrives because every member works for the common good. Players have set positions and areas they can and cannot go into. Everyone knows what they are doing and if they don't do what they are supposed to be doing within the team shape they will find themselves left back – left back in the changing room that is by a coach with no room for passengers.

Already sufficiently important to the side that he had been appointed captain before Klopp's arrival, Henderson's appreciation that the team comes first has seen him invariably give his all wherever he is asked to play. Instead of number 14 perhaps he should be number 40, rather like the WD40 that famously oils all moving parts keeping them working smoothly. At various times he has been asked to operate in a deep position. Sometimes he has been given licence to storm forward in a box to box midfielder's role or to play in a more advanced position.

Equally he has operated centrally or in wide berths on either flank and at times has even slotted into defence. Rather than making him a Jordan of all trades and master of none Hendo has been excellent in all of these positions. He always sees the big picture and plays for the good of the team ahead of himself, something more often noted by managers and colleagues than anyone else. His link up play with his team-mates at Liverpool illustrates the thought he puts into the game and the hours he puts in studying the nuances of every individual's game. Trent Alexander Arnold has rightly won many plaudits for the quality of his crosses which produce so many goals, but look again at those crosses and see how many times the full-back receives the ball from Hendo at just the right time and into just the right place.

While all this makes Jordan Jurgen's eyes and ears on the pitch, when Klopp arrived Hendo was out injured. No player likes being injured at any time, especially when a new manager comes into a club. For Henderson the injury was particularly badly timed especially considering the difficulty he had in establishing himself in Brendan Rodgers' thoughts when the previous boss breezed into Anfield. Throughout his career Hendo has been a model of consistency, sometimes playing more games than anyone else, but in the first of Klopp's campaigns Jordan was hit by a series of injuries.

Klopp took over four days after Rodgers' dismissal on 4 October 2015. Liverpool had played nine games under their new manager before Henderson made his comeback as a sub, two minutes after James Milner had slotted the only goal of a home win over Swansea from the penalty spot in late November. He had also missed the last nine matches of Rodgers' reign, having had almost three and a half months out altogether.

Having come in at the start of an international break and had the opportunity to work with the remainder of the squad not away with their countries the early weeks under Klopp had brought three draws, but improvement had come before Henderson was available. Other than a home defeat to a late goal at the hands of Crystal Palace five of the six games before Jordan's return had been won.

Klopp eased the skipper back into action, bringing him on for the last quarter of an hour when Liverpool were already 5-1 up in a Capital One Cup win at

Southampton but leaving him on the bench in a loss at Newcastle where Gini Wijnaldum wrapped up victory for the Magpies. A first start under Klopp came in the tamer surroundings of FC Sion in the Europa League where he played most of a goalless draw.

Jordan then marked his first Premier League start under Jurgen Klopp by opening the scoring in a game against West Brom where it needed a 95th minute deflected equaliser from Divock Origi to salvage a point. This saw Klopp erupt in wild celebrations that included beating his chest in the direction of Tony Pulis and co in the Albion dug out. There was no post-match handshake between the managers as for the first time Klopp took his side to the Kop to salute the fans. It had been an emotional afternoon and one in which the return of Hendo had given Liverpool more energy in the centre of the park, although had Klopp been able to bring himself on even Jordan might have had to play second fiddle.

Origi's equaliser prevented what would have been three Premier League defeats in a row as the follow up to the Albion revival was a tame 3-0 loss at Watford but a couple of 1-0 wins over Leicester and Sunderland steadied the ship. Jordan however limped out of his return to the Stadium of Light with a knock that caused him to miss three games just as he was getting back into the groove.

He had made the right impression with Klopp already and once fit was immediately back into the starting line-up against Arsenal at Anfield. From there he managed to stay fit and play regularly as Liverpool stayed in upper mid-table without being able to break into the top six. They did however reach the Capital One Cup final, losing 3-1 on penalties to Manchester City with Henderson yet to take one when the cup was lost.

Returning to regular football Jordan earned an England recall for a victory over world champions Germany in Berlin where from his near post corner Eric Dier scored a last minute winner. Still looking for his first full international goal Hendo had earlier looked a certain scorer when set up by his old mate Danny Welbeck only for his shot to strike a defender and go for a corner.

Two weeks later Jordan made a swift return to Germany as Klopp returned to Borussia Dortmund for a Europa League game, but after creating Liverpool's goal for Origi in a 1-1 draw Henderson was unable to take the field for the second half.

His injury strewn season once again stalled, this time through torn knee ligaments.

The injury kept him out for five weeks, returning as a second half sub in the final Premier League match of the season at West Brom, where a point saw Liverpool come to rest in eighth place, six points behind Wembley conquerors Manchester City in the final Champions League position.

There was still another cup final to play. Having staged a remarkable fight-back to beat Borussia Dortmund in the second leg of the game Hendo was injured in, Liverpool had progressed to the final of the Europa League where they met Unai Emery's Seville in Switzerland. Named on the bench Jordan had to collect his loser's medal after not playing. Having led at half time Liverpool found themselves chasing the game and though Klopp summoned a midfielder a couple of minutes after going 3-1 down it was Joe Allen, not Jordan, who got the call.

Four days after the final Hendo's focus had switched to England. With the European Championships in France coming up Jordan won his 24th cap as a sub against Turkey at Manchester City's Etihad Stadium. After helping England turn a draw into a victory four days later he returned to the starting line-up for England at his former home ground of the Stadium of Light, Marcus Rashford marking his debut with a third minute goal as England beat Australia 2-1.

Going into the Euros Jordan might have wondered about his place in the team for the finals. In the last warm-up game against Portugal at Wembley he only got off the bench in the last minute, as England defended a 1-0 lead given to them by Chris Smalling just three minutes earlier.

Hopes were high that England would excel at the Euros but it was to prove a struggle under former Liverpool boss Roy Hodgson. Having been brought on for Dele Alli to help see out the 1-0 warm up v Portugal perhaps Hodgson should have done the same in the opening match against Russia as Hendo sat out the match, watching England concede an equaliser two minutes into injury time, Hodgson having used only two of his subs.

Henderson remained an unused reserve in the next game too as Chris Coleman's over-achieving Wales were edged out as this time England scored in added time, sub Sturridge doing the damage. Hodgson decided to freshen up his side for the final group game against Slovakia, Hendo coming into the side and going close to breaking the deadlock in what proved to be a goalless draw, as he saw his volley deflected wide moments before the interval. The point edged England through to the knock-out stage at Slovakia's expense but Jordan found himself back on the bench kicking his heels for the entire game as England disastrously lost to Iceland despite taking the lead from a fourth minute penalty.

While the Euros were occupying the footballing public the restless Jurgen Klopp was preparing for his first full season at Liverpool. Before the end of the transfer window 14 players left the club in addition to a host of loans. Departures included Brendan Rodgers' midfield choice Joe Allen while through the in-door four of the six signings came from German football. Amongst these was Joel Matip from Schalke 04 while the signings from English clubs were Sadio Mane from Southampton and Dutch playmaker Gini Wijnaldum who had done well against Liverpool for Newcastle in the season just gone.

Following his extended season with England Hendo was given a late start, coming into the reckoning at the start of the International Champions Cup where he played against Chelsea, Milan, Roma and finally Barcelona in the final at Wembley. Hendo came on at half time against Barca and helped Liverpool to three of their four goals in a resounding 4-0 victory. That score-line was reversed with Jordan in the starting line-up as Klopp took his team to the first club he managed, Mainz 05, as an extensive pre-season build-up concluded with a reality check.

The season started with Henderson having had Klopp's backing as there was no question of his leadership qualities not resulting in his retention of the captaincy. It wasn't just the team that was developing under Klopp. The Main Stand development that brought Anfield's capacity up to 54,000 from 44,000 meant that the opening home game didn't come until after the first international break, the unveiling celebrated with a 4-1 win over Premier League champions Leicester.

The following fixture took Liverpool to Chelsea who would emerge as the new season's champions. Not only would Liverpool inflict their first defeat under new manager Antonio Conte, they would move into the top four and do so on the back of a sensational winner from Hendo, a goal so good it won the Carling Goal of the Month award. "It's definitely one of the best goals I've scored, if not the best," Jordan beamed. "As soon as it left my boot really I thought I had a chance."

With his usual ability to nail a moment Klopp described it as "A lifetime goal." It was a goal of genuine beauty. Latching onto an under-hit clearance from Gary Cahill, as he killed the ball with his instep, Henderson was doing so while looking not at the ball but measuring up his target some 30 yards away. With his second touch being one primarily concerned with placement rather than power he curled the ball right into the far top corner, beyond the dive of one of the world's best goalkeepers in Thibaut Courtois. It was the footballing equivalent of a hole in one and a goal any player on the planet would have been justifiably proud of.

It would be Jordan's only goal of a season that finished early. Until mid-February Henderson was ever present as Liverpool improved dramatically, even topping the table either side of a 6-1 firework display against Watford in early November. Having stayed in the top three until the end of January after a 2-0 home win over Tottenham Liverpool were fourth but just a point behind second placed Spurs, albeit Chelsea were disappearing at the top of the table.

Unfettered by cup distractions, having not qualified for Europe and now out of both domestic cups, having reached the semi-finals of the League Cup Liverpool were ready for an all-out assault on at least equalling their second spot finish of three seasons earlier. They would have to do it without their skipper.

Shortly after the big win over Spurs Jordan injured his foot in training. Initially it was believed the knock would only keep him out short-term but two months later he was still on crutches and would not play until the following campaign. The injury came at a time when not just the team but Jordan especially were playing well. He had responded with typical commitment to the role Klopp had carved out for him as a deep-lying 'number six.'

With some critics never far away, early doubters soon had to eat their keyboard warrior words as he had grown into the role, now driving the team forward more by his ability to dictate play than his sheer stamina. Not just his passing but his ability to choose the right ball and execute it quickly set the tone for Liverpool performances, a quality only noticed by some when he wasn't there.

Regardless of earlier years when he barely missed a game, or the fact that virtually every footballer gets injured at some point, there were questions asked over the summer of 2017 about whether as captain Jordan Henderson was going to be able to enjoy an injury free season after becoming too familiar with the medical room since taking over the captaincy. Nonetheless he had recovered for the start of the season and was able to play in the opening friendly on 12 July, a 4-0 win at Tranmere.

Hendo would play in all but the last of Liverpool's eight warm up matches, lifting the Premier League Asia Cup after beating Leicester in the final in Hong Kong but then being the only man to fail in the penalty shoot-out as the final of the Audi Cup was lost to Atletico Madrid in the Allianz Arena. The final friendly match against Athleico Bilbao in Dublin saw Henderson, Adam Lallana, Philippe Coutinho and Daniel Sturridge miss out, in Jordan's case through illness rather than injury.

Henderson was in the side the following weekend for the start of season at Watford and played every game – as well as returning to the England line-up – before being left on the bench in an October trip to Slovenia. Liverpool waltzed to a 7-0 first leg victory over Maribor, the biggest away win an English team had ever recorded in the European Cup / Champions League. Although he missed the odd game through squad rotation or, in the case of a Champions League game at Manchester City, through suspension, Henderson was available for almost all of the season barring a thigh injury that ruled him out of a win at West Ham in November and a month out from Christmas with a muscle injury that made him miss six games.

At that point tongues wagged about Henderson's ability to remain consistently available, conjuring up speculation that perhaps Sir Alex Ferguson's comments in his biography about Hendo's running style leading to problems as he got older had some validity in them. In truth come the end of the season Jordan had made mincemeat of that argument by playing a total of 53 games, including 12 for England, in a season where he reached the Champions League final and the World Cup semi-final.

Klopp's gegenpressing requires immense fitness. There's no point pressing hard for 80 minutes and then tiring and being caught out late on. Modern day footballers are supreme athletes but remain human after all and the Liverpool manager has been in the forefront of those criticising fixture lists that produce too fast turnarounds at busy periods. Jurgen is no-one's fool and in getting the best out of his team is prepared to rest key men. Consequently several of the games where

Hendo didn't play were simply because he was being rested, even if that meant having him as an unused sub in case required, such as in the home Champions League fixture with Spartak Moscow. On that occasion a 7-0 score-line was run up with Hendo kept fresh for the following weekend's Merseyside derby where he was straight back in the starting XI.

This was a season where Liverpool stepped up. The 44 goals and 14 assists of the phenomenal Mo Salah rightly occupied the headline writers and excited the fans but not even a player in such form as Salah was that year can make a team, and as always Henderson's priority was helping to make the team tick. Klopp's first full season had seen Liverpool qualify for the Champions League for the first time in three seasons but in a year where they hadn't also had to contend with any kind of European campaign. In Klopp's second full season not only did the Reds reach the final of the Champions League they also qualified for the following season's competition via their Premier League position. It was the first time they had achieved consecutive top four finishes since 2009. Given the success that came of that European qualification the Anfield win over Brighton on the last day of the Premier League campaign should be seen as of comparable importance to the Champions League final that followed it.

Klopp has to take great credit for keeping his team on track despite major upheaval in the January transfer window. During Jordan's absence at the turn of the year Liverpool lost the magician of Coutinho who went to Barcelona for over £100m but they succeeded in signing Virgil van Dijk from Southampton for £75m. Klopp called his team together as the magician made himself disappear to tell them that allowing their season to come off the rails because Coutinho had gone would only allow critics to say they had been a one-man team. The irony of this in a side based on collective rather than individual strength would not have been lost on Hendo in particular, being the ultimate team player. Moreover, as good as Coutinho is, and he was nothing short of brilliant at Liverpool, world class attackers always seem to be more plentiful than world class defenders. In Vincent Kompany Manchester City had a defender who could make a difference and in acquiring Van Dijk Liverpool added their own defensive king-pin.

Van Dijk came into the Champions League line up after Liverpool had emerged as unbeaten group winners. The Dutchman debuted at this level as a Sadio Mane hat-trick produced a stunning 5-0 away win at Porto on a night when Henderson was brought off shortly after Bobby Firmino made it 4-0 with 20 minutes left.

Having eased through the goalless second leg the quarter-final tie paired Liverpool with Manchester City. Neither Van Dijk or Henderson had been involved when City were beaten 4-3 at Anfield in January. Two late goals that day brought Pep Guardiola's side back from the dead but this time with both Virgil and Jordan playing Liverpool were solid at the back and established a firm 3-0 lead to take down the M62 for the second leg. Blitzing City with the sort of rapid fire start that has come to destroy even quality opposition, that three goal lead was in place by the 31st minute but try as they might there was no way City could get one away goal, never mind three.

Former Red Raheem Sterling set up Gabriel Jesus to score just two minutes into the second leg to raise hopes of a blue moon but Liverpool went on to score twice in the second half to emphatically win 5-1 on aggregate. City grumbled about a disallowed goal just before half time, Guardiola being sent to the stands after going too far with his protests.

In the league City had scored those two late goals at Anfield to narrow a 4-1 scoreline to 4-3. In the semi-final of the Champions League Roma would score twice in the last 10 minutes at Anfield to retrieve a slight chance of progress after Liverpool had roared into a five-goal lead. Roma's goalkeeper Alisson would have better nights at Anfield. Former I Giallorossi man Mo Salah destroyed his old team – although he celebrated neither of his goals. Salah set Liverpool on the way with the first two strikes, the opener coming after Henderson began the move by dispossessing Manchester City old boy Edin Dzeko.

Liverpool's worrying habit of leaking late goals apparently having switched off thinking the game was won surfaced again in the second leg in Rome. Radja Nainggolan scored twice after the 86th minute to provide some late worries that should have been impossible after Sadio Mane's early goal extended the aggregate lead to 6-2 only for Liverpool to finally edge through 7-6. "We never do it the easy way unfortunately" breathed Jordan straight after the final whistle, "Amazing effort. We knew it would be tough. We did well, scored some good goals. Overall I thought we handled the situation well apart from maybe the last 10 minutes of the second half, conceding two goals. We need to stop that."

In the lead up to the final Liverpool city centre was awash with street stalls selling Champions League final merchandise, most of it featuring Mo Salah. It was to be destination Kiev where Henderson would captain Liverpool in a classic Champions League final against Real Madrid.

The ecstasy of winning the Champions League in 2019 was heightened by losing in the final of 2018, not that it seemed like that on the occasion of the 3-1 defeat to Real. The game hinged on three things: a first half shoulder injury that saw the withdrawal of star scorer Salah, a goal as good as any ever seen in a European final by Gareth Bale and a goalkeeping performance that contained two costly howlers by Liverpool's Loris Karius.

24-year old Karius endured a nightmare with two calamities in the biggest club game of all with the world watching. If ever a man walked alone on a football pitch it was Karius after that match. To 2020 he has not played for Liverpool again, having had two years in Turkish football on loan to Besiktas. Interviewed on the pitch immediately after the game skipper Hendo tried to stand up for his colleague. Put to Jordan that while goalkeepers' errors are always magnified there had been two bad mistakes by Karius, Jordan said, "The first one I didn't really know what happened." Looking puzzled, he added " I wasn't sure if it was allowed or if it had been blocked with his hands. The overhead kick he can do nothing. The third one obviously the ball's got loads of movement on so it's always difficult. It's not about him and the mistakes he might have made. It's about us as a team. We got here together as a team and we lose as a team as well. We're all in it together. It's not about one person, it's about everybody and we just weren't good enough on the night to get over the line but I'm so proud of all the players and the fans came out in their numbers again so we've got to thank them and I hope we can keep going now and get into more finals."

Obviously massively disappointed, Jordan kept his composure throughout that on-pitch interview. Loyally speaking up for a teammate who had made two monumental mistakes, as always Hendo looked to the positives and to the future, adding, "We've got a fantastic squad and a fantastic manager and we've got to use this to keep going forward. Obviously it's going to hurt for a while but football moves forward. The World Cup is coming and then the season starts really fast after that."

No matter how deep the disappointment Jordan is a player who will never shirk an interview or mutter a few snappily brief answers if pushed into fulfilling media obligations. Communicating with the fans is something he does as naturally as communicating with his teammates during a game. Analysing the final he observed, "It's disappointing of course. We did well to get the goal and get back in the game but there were mistakes. Madrid were really good. We knew they were a fantastic side and they were always going to hurt you. They deserved to win. They were obviously the better team on the night but I felt, especially in the first half, [particularly] the first 30-35 minutes we dominated with the ball and had a couple of chances. It's frustrating obviously but you have got to give credit to Madrid. When Mo got injured they started dominating a little bit more with the ball...we stayed in the game, we got the goal back and we still believed that we could go on but there were a couple of goals which on another night wouldn't have gone in."

As the Liverpool squad pulled out of the NSC Olimpiyskiy Stadium in Kiev Zinedine Zidane had joined Carlo Ancelotti and Bob Paisley as part of the select managerial trio to have won the European Cup / Champions League three times. Born in Hetton, Paisley originated just over three miles away from Herrington born Henderson. Jordan left the Ukrainian capital of Kiev a loser but would have his Champions League triumph a year later. Before then he had the World Cup to contemplate. The tournament started fewer than three weeks after the curtain came down on his club campaign.

Captaining the country in the final warm-up game for the FIFA World Cup finals as Costa Rica were beaten in Leeds, Jordan played the full game as Gareth Southgate's side started what would be a thrilling run with a 2-1 win over Tunisia in Volgograd on the day after Jordan's 28th birthday.

Henderson started five of England's seven games at the finals, being an unused sub in the third place play-off and the final group game lost to Belgium after qualification was already guaranteed. Having played the full 90 minutes in all the games he played, Hendo was hooked by Southgate seven minutes into extra-time of the semi-final against Croatia with the score level, Mario Mandzukic's winner coming after he left the field still dreaming of a place in the final. Ultimately Jordan ended a high class season with nothing tangible other than a loser's medal, but with the experience gained of playing through to the final of the Champions League and the semi-final of the World Cup.

Liverpool certainly recognised the level their skipper had reached and rewarded Jordan with a new long-term contract which he put pen to paper to on 3 September, saying, "I'm very happy to have signed a new contract for a long period of time. I'm absolutely delighted. It doesn't seem like too long ago when I signed my first one – it feels like yesterday, really – but a lot has happened since then. I feel it's been a progressive journey for me throughout my time here and one I've enjoyed so much. There is no other place in the world I would rather play football. I want to be here for as long as I can be. I'm so privileged to have been a part of this club for so long, and hopefully even longer now."

Given his summer exertions Jordan was not used in pre-season until the last 20 minutes of the ninth and final friendly against Torino at Anfield, coming off the bench at the same point a week later as the Premier League got going with a statement victory over West Ham. By now Liverpool had solved their goalkeeping problem by bringing in arguably the world's best goalkeeper in Brazilian Alisson from Roma. Also debuting that day was former Stoke star Xherdan Shaqiri and, most notably for Hendo, Naby Keita.

Keita's arrival was not a surprise, the £48m deal for a player described by Klopp as the 'complete midfielder' having been lined up a year earlier. Liverpool had patiently waited for a release clause from RB Leipzig to become valid. As expected competition for a place in the ambitious Champions League finalists XI was fierce and Keita's addition would simply become another challenge for every midfielder including Henderson.

Keita started the first three Premier League games all of which were won without a goal being conceded as Hendo was eased back in. Knowing another long hard season was ahead Klopp used his skipper sparingly early on, Jordan coming off the bench for the final quarter of each game, the third of those for Keita.

Although Liverpool had gone to the top of the table after those opening games the performance in a 1-0 Anfield win over Brighton had been disjointed. With a step up in the quality of opposition coming up with a trip to Leicester Henderson was back in the starting line-up a couple of days before signing his new contract, this time Keita replacing Hendo in the final quarter. The 100% record was maintained despite a blunder from the expensive new keeper Alisson giving Leicester a way back into the game after Liverpool had gone two up.

Back on the bench for a Wembley win over Spurs, when after coming on he briefly played alongside Keita, Jordan played his first full 90 minutes of the season as the Champions League campaign kicked off with a thrilling 3-2 home win over star-studded PSG. The footnote to that game was the added time debut of Fabinho, the Brazilian international whose ability to offer a patrolling presence in front of the defence would lead to a change of role for skipper Henderson. That was yet to come however and four days after his first 90 minutes there was another full game for Hendo in a convincing home victory over Southampton.

The start of the season had seen 17 goals scored and just four conceded as the first seven games were all won but a home defeat to Chelsea in the League Cup broke the spell. Just two goals were scored in four winless games, when two losses could have been three but for Riyad Mahrez failing with a late Manchester City penalty at Anfield.

At this point Henderson was having to work hard for his place in competition with Keita. The pair often coming on as substitute for each other and rarely playing together, while for a spell around Halloween both Hendo and Keita were unavailable for just short of three weeks due to injury.

As the season progressed, while the attacking triumvirate of Salah, Mane and Firmino were totally established as the first choice front three, in midfield Klopp employed more of a rotation system. Perhaps this was down to the energy his engine room have to expend in a system where the final ball most often comes from wing-backs Alexander-Arnold and Robertson, but for Hendo and company it was more of a challenge to be in the team.

The first 17 games of 2019 brought a dozen different midfield combinations, the most common starting three of Hendo, Milner and Wijnaldum beginning together just three times in that period. With Fabinho often excelling in the 'No 6' role Jordan found himself often being used more in the way he had played under Brendan Rodgers, using his running power as a box to box player.

After coming on as substitute to make one and score one in a 3-1 win at Southampton, Jordan played exceptionally well in a Champions League win over

Porto operating in a more advanced role than the '6' position he had become synonymous with under Klopp. Typically in that Porto match it had been Jordan's understanding with Trent Alexander-Arnold which had fed the wing-back in the build-up to Bobby Firmino's goal which added to Keita's early opener.

Speaking to liverpoolfc.com's Sam Williams Jordan revealed he'd had a discussion with Jurgen about his role in the team, "Me and the gaffer just had a conversation. Obviously he saw the England games. [Hendo had been given licence to attack more by the inclusion of Eric Dier in a recent win over the Czech Republic and had then marked his 50th cap with a masterful assist for a Raheem Sterling goal in a big win in Montenego.] I felt good playing in that position. I felt more natural and it was something he said he would think about. I can do both positions and he sees I can do both. It's basically what he wants and needs. I feel more comfortable and natural in that position for England, creating chances further up and doing what I enjoy doing. At the same time when I played number six I felt I've learned that position really well. I don't think the manager had thought about it too much until I mentioned it to him...the manager might not have seen me in that position too much. It's all about putting the team first, I know that but at the same time I want to contribute as much as I can. I feel as though I can do that more in a position further forward.

"In the last couple of years there hasn't really been a player like Fabinho in that role, so I've had to adapt to that role. I think I've done quite well. I think if you look at Fab, it's quite natural to him. That's his position and he's so good at what you need to do in that position. I just thought that might give me a bit more license to get forward more. The manager wants me in both positions, which is good for me and the team."

This was an unusual interview from Henderson and maybe indicated he felt he needed to speak up for himself a bit more. Not so much to the manager who he evidently enjoys a mutual respect with but to the public via the club's website. Not one to normally praise himself, the comments about thinking he had done quite well in the six role highlighted how he saw his value there while recognising that role was under threat from Fabinho's excellence. Similarly while his mantra of putting the team first is referred to the addition of, 'but at the same time I want to contribute as much as I can' and putting himself forward for a more attacking role was perhaps slightly out of character. Not that there's anything wrong with that. Jordan has always been honest in his assessments, if anything being particularly modest about his own attributes.

Indeed he once told the Mail's Oliver Holt, "I don't like reading good things about myself. With the criticism and the negative things, I always think that makes me better. You need a little bit of good now and again but the good for me comes from the manager. That's the good I enjoy, so if I'm told I'm doing my job right, brilliant. Anything outside of that, I tend not to get involved. I'm not particularly into people giving me credit. It's not something I think about. It's not important to me. The only thing that's important is if I'm doing my job properly on the pitch for the team and for the manager. I try to leave that to other people. I prefer talking about how well others are doing because that's what I want. That's what I try to do as a captain: give them a platform where they can go and perform as best they can. I can always accept criticism. Throughout my career, I've always had criticism and I think that's good. Criticism's healthy. It gives you that extra little bit inside you to prove people wrong, to use it as energy, to use it as fuel."

Nonetheless there were plenty of good things rightly being said and written about Liverpool. At this point they had given themselves a great chance of reaching the semi-finals of the Champions League and were in a two horse race for the Premier League title with Manchester City. As Porto were being beaten at Anfield the table showed Liverpool two points ahead of City with fifteen points for Liverpool to play for but 18 still available to Guardiola's men. Neither side dared drop a point and with City holding a seven goal superiority in goal difference there was the added pressure of having to not only win but win well as the destination of the trophy may well have come down to goal difference.

The following weekend brought third placed Chelsea to Liverpool where the Reds kept rolling on with a 2-0 victory as City won 3-1 on the same day at Crystal Palace. The second leg of the Champions League quarter-final at Porto saw Klopp go for a midfield three of Fabinho, Milner and Wijnaldum who came back into the team after a couple of games out. With a two goal cushion on a ground where they had won 5-0 the season before Liverpool were always in control with Hendo coming off the bench to make his mark with an assist for fellow sub Firmino as a 6-1 aggregate win was ramped up.

Despite Barcelona lying in wait in the semi-final Liverpool simply had to keep churning out results in the Premier League and did so without conceding a goal in wins at Cardiff and at home to bottom of the pile Huddersfield, Henderson putting in the full 180 minutes. Unfortunately City kept winning, hopes that they might drop points against Spurs – who had just knocked them out of the Champions League - or Manchester United proving unfounded.

With Fabinho playing as No 6, Keita got the nod ahead of the captain for the eagerly awaited semi-final with Barca at the Nou Camp, James Milner completing the midfield. Hendo however was quickly into the action, coming on in the 24th minute as Keita hobbled off. Barely had Jordan had a chance to consider the pace of the game than his side went behind – Luis Suarez the scorer of the home side's 500th Champions League goal.

It simply wasn't Liverpool's night as they equalled their record Champions League defeat, losing 3-0. In form Mane – with 15 goals in his last 18 games – blasted over from eight yards after a great ball from Henderson. Late on Lionel Messi seemed to take the tie away from Klopp's class of 2019 by scoring twice, the second a sumptuous free kick that was his 600th goal for the club 14 years to the day since his first!

"I still can't believe he scored it. I actually thought he was going to take it short" reflected Henderson later, "Messi put that shot in the one area Ali [Alisson] couldn't protect. The whip, the pace, the precision -- it was absolutely perfect." Speaking to the Daily Mail Jordan revealed a lesson he had learned from the man who gave him his senior debut, Roy Keane.

Liverpool's phenomenal fightback against Barcelona was still to come. Keane himself knew something about Champions League semi-final fightbacks. Twenty years earlier his performance after helping Manchester United to overcome Juventus after receiving a yellow card that had ruled him out of the final, if United got there, was the stuff of legend. Not for Roy the Gazza like tears after he was carded at Italia 90. Instead he steered his side to the final leaving his manager Sir Alex Ferguson to later describe it as, "The most emphatic display of selflessness I have seen on a football field. Pounding over every blade of grass, competing as if he would rather die of exhaustion than lose. He inspired all around him. I felt such an honour to be associated with such a player."

Rather like Jordan Henderson not liking to read praise of himself Roy Keane was distinctly unimpressed. "Stuff like that almost insults me. What am I supposed to do? Give up? Not cover every blade of grass? Not do my best for my teammates? Not do my best for my club? I actually get offended when people throw quotes like that at me, as if I'm supposed to be honoured by it. It's like praising the postman for delivering your letters. He's supposed to isn't he? That's his job."

Keane had evidently had an influence on Henderson. "It was the first time I had been on a pitch with Lionel Messi' he explained of that meeting in the Nou Camp. "You don't think to yourself 'Oh my God -- that's him,' but there's no question he plays the game differently to when you see him on TV. He's so fast. Did I think about asking for his shirt? No. I've never done it. Roy Keane told me when I was at Sunderland that if you ask for someone's shirt, it looks like you are in awe of them. Evidently Hendo wasn't in awe of the magical Messi as he had played against him before. They were on the pitch together for 30 minutes at Wembley in the pre-season Champions Cup in 2016.

Jordan did collect a souvenir of that trip to Barcelona. "As it turned out, I came home with Luis Suárez's shirt. Luis is a good lad and he gave me it as a gesture as we had played together for Liverpool" he explained before adding a touch of self-deprecation by quipping, "I don't know what he's done with mine!"

It would have been Liverpool shirts that were most valued after the second leg. The previous season Barca had seen a 4-1 score-line not prove good enough as they went to Roma and were eliminated on away goals after losing 3-0. So despite their commanding lead, illustrious personnel and vast experience they had to come to Anfield knowing that a Liverpool European night was not a forgone conclusion, as much as they wanted to be able to strut their stuff in the final in Madrid.

In between the two-legs of the semi-final with there was a trip back to Hendo's native north-east but one with a Spanish flavour as the trip to Tyneside brought Liverpool up against the last manager to win the Champions League with Liverpool. A late Divock Origi goal edged a five goal thriller with Rafa Benitez's Newcastle before Liverpool attempted the sort of comeback against Barcelona that Benitez had shown was possible one night in Istanbul.

It wasn't just at St. James' that Origi showed he was ready to add to the established front three and be part of a Fab Four. The last time a team had overcome a three goal first leg deficit in a semi-final of European football's premier competition had come almost a decade before Origi was born. On that occasion in 1986 Barcelona had come from behind to knock out Gothenburg. With only Mane of the first choice attack playing Origi got the night off to a great start by getting one goal back after only seven minutes, tapping home after a well-timed burst by Hendo had forced ter-Stegen to parry his shot into Origi's path.

Still in control of the tie the Catalonian club went in at half time still 3-1 up on aggregate and knowing with a line-up that included Liverpool old boys Suarez and Coutinho, as well as Lionel Messi, they were always likely to add an away goal.

There have been many special European nights at Anfield. This one even surpassed the David Fairclough 'Super-sub' quarter-final against St. Etienne in 1977. Almost 10 minutes into the second half the might of Barcelona crumbed under a wall of noise tumbling not just from the Kop but the whole of Anfield – barring the Catalonians' corner. Twice in the space of 122 magical seconds substitute Georginio Wijnaldum scored to bring the tie level with over a third of the game still to go.

This was knife edge football. Liverpool had Barca on the ropes but one attack could rejuvenate the visitors if they scored to leave Liverpool needing not one but two more goals. Jurgen's juggernaut had to keep going forward but do so in a controlled sense. There were 34 minutes to go after Wijnaldum's equaliser, not 34 seconds. With Jordan driving that juggernaut sooner or later that winner would come, Origi providing the knock-out blow with a jabbed finish from the cutest of disguised corners from Alexander-Arnold.

"It was amazing. A special one for everyone really. For the fans, the team, everyone. I'm not sure that people expected it before the game but we said to each other we would fight right until the end and give everything. We managed to do that tonight." A justifiably broad grin broke out on Jordan's face as he continued, "Thankfully we managed to score four and keep a clean sheet which was what was needed so I'm so proud of the lads for what they've done tonight and what they've achieved." Despite that grin, typically Hendo was already thinking ahead rather than wallowing in the afterglow. Quickly he added, "At the same time it's a semi-final and now we need to go to a final and we need to win."

Interviewed by the always insightful Simon Crabtree, it was put to Hendo that while he always had hope, had he had genuine belief that the team could beat Barcelona by four goals? "I know it's easy to say now but within the team there was always belief" insisted the skipper. "That's the great thing about this team. The manager always believes. You could see that in the talk he gave before we came to the stadium. That helped the players believe and you could see that from the first minute in the game. We started well, got a good goal and from then on kept believing, kept fighting, and got our rewards in the end."

Everyone had given everything. Every player, supporter and staff member was drained. If Roy Keane had covered every blade of grass in Manchester United's 1999 semi-final with Juventus, Jordan Henderson had covered every blade of Anfield twice. At the final whistle a player who routinely puts absolutely everything into every match, not just the big ones, collapsed on the pitch. Jordan was unable to move until Joe Gomez came and picked his captain up.

Part of the emotional outpouring was caused by events in Manchester the previous evening. City's 1-0 win over Leicester had deposed Liverpool from the Premier League pinnacle they had occupied for most of the season. With just one game left City now topped the table, a point clear. While two goals from Sadio Mane tamed Wolves the following weekend City's 4-1 win at Brighton came as no surprise, even though the Seagulls had taken the lead. Liverpool were 25 points clear of third placed Chelsea. That was no consolation but what was a consolation was that having been 25 points behind City the previous season Liverpool had narrowed the gap to just one. They knew they could overtake City the following year. What's more, City knew it too and the pressure would tell on them.

In the meantime Jordan and Jurgen had another Champions League final to prepare for. That final of course would see Jordan lift the trophy after guiding his team to triumph over Tottenham as we saw in chapter two. That and the Premier League title which followed it is the blossoming of the Jordan and Jurgen journey that still has some way to go.

Now a vintage red, Henderson has developed into legendary status under Klopp. Still under-appreciated by some, there is no denying the simple fact that Jordan has joined Emlyn Hughes, Phil Thompson, Graeme Souness and Steven Gerrard as one of the five figures in history to have captained Liverpool to the Champions League / European Cup.

From the starting point that he was doing so well he was already Liverpool's captain, Henderson's game has reached new levels under Klopp. From a young age Jordan was much more tactically aware than most of his contemporaries. The German manager's tightly disciplined team structure has utilised Hendo's ability to see things quickly and act upon them to the immense benefit of the team. Liverpool are a team full of top stars and Henderson is far from the only great character in the side, but undeniably Liverpool are a better team when Henderson plays. He helps everyone else play. He leads by example as well as being a vocal leader. From the days as a youngster when he was nut-megging Paul Scholes to the times when he didn't want to swap shirts with Lionel Messi Henderson has always been entirely single-minded. Stubbornly determined with an intrinsic sense of self-motivation that gives the skipper a mentality which rubs off on those around him. Like all good captains he gets that little bit extra out of the teammates around him.

Klopp has called his team 'Mentality Monsters'. In a world of Van Dijk, Salah, Firmino, Mane and co. Hendo is the biggest mentality monster of them all.

## CHAPTER TEN

# ENGLAND

Jordan was only 12 when he made his first appearance at an England international – as a ball boy. "I can remember the atmosphere being really good and it was amazing for me to be so close to the pitch and watch it first hand, watching these top players like Rooney, Beckham, people like that, I think Stevie [Gerrard] might have played too. It was a special night for me to be able to be there and part of it." Jordan remembered of an occasion when England beat Turkey 2-0 in a key Euro 2004 qualifier at Sunderland's Stadium of Light in April 2003. Goals from Darius Vassell and an added time David Beckham penalty gave England a 2-0 on a night when Gerrard did indeed win his 15th cap.

Being a ball boy because that international happened to take place at the club where he played for the academy was Jordan's only experience of international football until he went on loan to Coventry. Not for him the development through the ranks of Under 15 internationals upwards. It was as an 18 year old Jordan first earned international recognition. During his loan with the Sky Blues he started a goalless draw with the Czech Republic at Walsall but was substituted and won just that single cap at Under 19 level.

Similarly for the Under 20s there would be just one appearance. August 2009 saw him come on as a sub for Watford's Ross Jenkins in a 5-0 win over Montenegro at West Brom. The game was a warm up for the Under 20 World Cup which started in Egypt the following month, but as England finished bottom of their group Jordan was otherwise occupied playing regularly in the Premier League. Four days before Brian Eastick's England commenced their campaign in Egypt Hendo was scoring his first goal for Sunderland in a Carling Cup tie against Birmingham.

Stepping up to the Under 21s in the summer of 2010 Hendo got a debut in a Friendly win over Uzbekistan at Bristol City's Ashton Gate. He then impressed as England won with a Daniel Sturridge goal in a UEFA Under 21 Championship preliminary game away to Portugal. The next international break brought Jordan's first international goal. Like his first club goal it came at Norwich City.

After playing in a comfortable win over Lithuania at Colchester Hendo hit a volley from outside the box to open the scoring in a 2-1 win over Romania at Carrow Road before helping England to a goalless draw in the return match four days later.

Henderson's form for his club combined with impressive displays with the Under 21s meant that a mere 20 months after sporting the three lions for the first time in front of fewer than four thousand people at Walsall he was playing before a full house at Wembley as the full national side took on France. Called up by Fabio Capello who had recently witnessed Jordan impressing with Sunderland, the 20-year old as usual put heart and soul into his game but spent most of the time chasing the ball rather than being on it. Asked to partner Gareth Barry as one of two holding midfielders Hendo was the only player to pick up a yellow card.

The reviews weren't great. Kevin McCarra, writing in the Guardian praised debutant Andy Carroll but observed. "It was worse for the other newcomer Jordan Henderson, who was in defensive midfield while lacking the know-how to check the victors." Writing for the BBC website, their Chief football writer Phil McNulty said, "Sunderland's Henderson endured a difficult night" although at least adding "but so did many of his more experienced team-mates." In the Telegraph, "Anonymous on his debut" was Henry Winter's assessment of Hendo. Nonetheless his energy in trying to restrict a slick French side saw Capello keep the youngster on for the full 90 minutes in a game where his partner Barry was one of five men withdrawn as England went down 2-1.

It would be 18 months until Henderson was capped again. By then Capello had been replaced by Roy Hodgson and Henderson was playing for Liverpool. During the intervening period, having had a taste of the quality of full international football Jordan continued his education in the Under 21s. A further 11 caps were acquired at that level before he returned to the big stage.

Stepping down to the Under 21s from the full team can be seen as a step back by many. In typical fashion Jordan viewed it as an opportunity rather than a slight, marking his return with a goal in a 4-0 win against Denmark in Viborg in March 2011. Still only 20, a player once viewed as lacking physicality showed his developing strength to outmuscle centre-back Andreas Bjelland and coolly slot the ball beyond future Everton goalkeeper Jonas Lossl.

Henderson would return to Denmark with the Under 21s in the summer for the UEFA Under 21 Championship finals. After playing in a warm-up win against Norway in Southampton, seven days later he played in a 1-1 draw with Spain in England's opening game of the finals having been transferred from Sunderland to Liverpool in between. It was a month of ups and downs for Hendo. The excitement of the move to Anfield was tempered by England disappointingly crashing out of the tournament. Another draw with Ukraine was followed by a 2-1 defeat to the Czech Republic, with Jordan's 21st birthday having been celebrated between the last two games.

2011-12 brought six Under 21 appearances on top of the 48 games he would play in his first season with Liverpool. These would include a 6-0 win over Azerbaijan at Watford; in which Hendo found the net along with his old youth team colleague from Sunderland Martyn Waghorn, and a 3-0 win over Iceland in Reykjavik in which his future Liverpool colleague Alex Oxlade-Chamberlain claimed a hat-trick.

Despite being Liverpool's Young Player of the year and having played more for the club than anyone else during the season Henderson had come in from plenty of criticism from supporters and reporters yet to be convinced he was the real deal. Although imminent Liverpool manager Brendan Rodgers would be amongst the many who had their doubts about the midfielder, former Liverpool boss Roy Hodgson had seen enough – and had enough good reports from his attitude and form for the Under 21s – to bring Hendo back into the full England squad.

With Frank Lampard injured for the summer's European Championships in Poland and the Ukraine Henderson was given special permission to be accepted into England's squad. Jordan had won his second full cap, and first as a Liverpool man, as a 73rd minute substitute for Gareth Barry in a 1-0 win over Norway in Oslo in late May and followed that up with a seven minute cameo at Wembley against Belgium in the final warm-up match.

There was a similar seven minute stint in the opening match of the finals as he came on to help secure a point in a 1-1 draw with France in Donetsk but wasn't called upon as England edged narrow wins over Sweden and joint hosts Ukraine to progress to the quarter-finals.

Delighted to be included in the squad and to have got on against France Hendo inevitably was itching to play and got his chance four minutes into extra time of the quarter-final with Italy in Kiev. Replacing Scott Parker, Jordan came on to partner Stevie G in the centre of a four man midfield. The game however remained stubbornly locked at 0-0 and after the Ashleys of Young and Cole failed from the spot England were out.

Although it was disappointing to lose, especially on penalties as England have so often, Jordan had got back into the England squad, played in a major tournament and played in two cup finals in his first season with Liverpool. Having turned 22 in between his two appearances at the Euros he would be almost 23 and a half by the time he would be called up by England again.

The 17-month gap until cap number six arrived in the FA's 150th Year celebration match with Chile wasn't helped by his ongoing battle to fight for his place at Liverpool as Brendan Rodgers initially looked to offload him.

While out of the full international picture Jordan remained young enough to still qualify for the Under 21s and a year on from Euro 2012 elimination against Italy found himself up against Italian opposition again, this time in the European Under 21 Championship finals in Israel where he captained his country having earlier in the year won the inaugural England Under 21 Player of the Year award.

It was to be a disastrous tournament for Stuart Pearce's side who lost all three games. Italy started the rot with a 1-0 win in Tel Aviv, Lorenzo Insigne getting the goal. Better was expected from the meetings with Norway and Israel but 3-1 and 1-0 defeats meant Pearce left his role at the end of the month after six years in charge. Jordan had started the first two matches, coming off the bench in the third with England already out. It would be Hendo's farewell to the Under 21 set-up as well as Pearce's. Jordan had played 27 times as an under 21 international, scoring four times.

At this point, a matter of days before he turned 23, the time for talk of potential and being one for the future was over. This was the third summer in a row Jordan had been to a major finals. At club level he had demonstrated to Brendan Rodgers he was worthy of a place at Liverpool. It was time to step up another level and in 2013-14 he would do that.

Recalled by England for that November 2013 game by Chile where he played the final 19 minutes, four days later he got on 15 minutes earlier against Germany, both Wembley games ending in 1-0 defeats. By the time of England's next fixture in March Hendo's form saw him in the starting line-up for the first time since his debut as a Sunderland player. Although Daniel Sturridge headed the only goal of that 1-0 home win over Denmark five minutes after Jordan was replaced with 13 minutes to go that was largely immaterial to Jordan's growing stature and when England next played again almost two months later he was again in the starting XI, playing the full game in a 3-0 win over Peru.

Once again Henderson's timing on the international scene was immaculate. Just as he had bounced back onto the scene ahead of Euro 2012 when he went to the finals as Lampard limped out, now he was part of the England scene ahead of the 2014 FIFA World Cup in Brazil. The difference was now he didn't need to rely on an injury to someone else to get into the squad. By now Jordan was increasingly understood as an influential figure at Liverpool. They had narrowly missed out on the title with Hendo's late season suspension after his red card against Manchester City held to be crucial.

Having taken his total of England caps into double figures with his 10th and 11th caps against Ecuador and Honduras in the build-up to Brazil Jordan was in the starting XI for the opening match amidst the humidity and heat of Manaus. Once again the opposition were Italy and once again England came off second best, Henderson being substituted late on as England lost 2-1.

As usual Jordan's birthday was celebrated away from home in the middle of a major tournament but equally as usual there was to be no birthday present for him. Two days after turning 24 he saw his clubmate Luis Suarez score twice as Uruguay defeated England 2-1. With Costa Rica beating Italy England were out of the tournament after just two games for the first time since 1958, a fact made no better by the goalless draw against Costa Rica that ended the trip, Hendo watching that one from the bench.

That dead rubber against the Costa Ricans would be the only one in a run of nine internationals between June and November that Jordan didn't start. Once again England were on the road to tournament qualification. Hosting Slovenia in

November they won their European Championship qualifying game 3-1 but only after coming back from a Henderson own goal when Jordan got his head to a free-kick from Milivoje Novakovic's free-kick and diverted the ball beyond Joe Hart.

Despite being benched for a 3-1 Friendly victory over Scotland at Celtic Park next time out Hendo started the next competitive fixture in the spring, as he would the remaining three games of the season.

An injury hit 2015-16 meant a nine month interlude between caps 22 and 23. Hendo's return saw him set up the winner for Eric Dier with an added time corner as England beat Germany 3-2 in Berlin. Two months later – having played as a substitute against Turkey in between – there would be another special occasion for Jordan as he lined up against Australia in his home town of Sunderland. "To me Sunderland is home and it's always been special" he admitted, "Football is massive here and we have very passionate fans. When I went to Liverpool I felt it was similar, how everyone is very close-knit but really passionate about football."

Helping England to a 2-1 Wearside win looked to stand Hendo in good stead for the forthcoming European championships but coming on in the last minute of the final pre-tournament rehearsal against Portugal at the Etihad did not augur well. For the finals in France he watched from the side-lines as four points were taken from a draw with Russia in Marseille and a narrow win over Wales in Lens.

Jordan was brought then brought into the side for the closing group game with Slovakia at Saint Etienne but although England had 29 efforts on goal – their most in a game at a tournament finals since 1980 – they couldn't score and drew 0-0. It was to be Jordan's only appearance at the finals. A week later he remained an unused sub as England woefully lost 2-1 to Iceland in Nice, Hodgson choosing Jack Wilshere as the midfielder he brought off the bench in addition to strikers Jamie Vardy and Marcus Rashford.

As Hendo had played at Sunderland just before the finals Sam Allardyce had steered the Black Cats to a strong end to the season. England turned to Big Sam following Hodgson's departure. Allardyce would have only one match in charge of the national side. Taking his team to Slovakia for a 2018 World Cup qualification match Allardyce included Henderson in midfield albeit he brought him off for Dele Alli after just over an hour with Adam Lallana's late winner giving Big Sam what would prove to be the shortest 100% record possible. Stung by a media investigation in which he ridiculed his predecessor and was accused of offering advice on circumventing FA rules on third party ownership – something he strongly denied -Big Sam left his job by mutual consent.

Had Allardyce remained in charge of the national side it would have been good news for Henderson. Jordan's Rolls-Royce engine would have impressed Big Sam but the appointment of Gareth Southgate was perhaps even better news for Hendo. From the beginning of 2011 Southgate had been the FA's head of elite development and had kept a keen eye on the development of Jordan and the group of young talent coming through in the intervening years including those he had mentored as Under 21 manager having succeeded Stuart Pearce.

Not only did Jordan start Southgate's first four games, he captained England in two of them. Having set up both of England's goals in a 2-0 Wembley win over Malta in the World Cup qualifier that commenced Southgate's reign, Jordan was given the honour of captaining England for the first time in the next qualifier. The game on 11 October 2016 was a goalless draw with Slovenia in Ljubljana. Jordan played the full game but handed the armband to Wayne Rooney when the veteran came on as sub with just over quarter of an hour left. Rooney would skipper England for the last time in the next game as Hendo played in a convincing 3-0 home win over Scotland as Southgate's World Cup campaign continued without a goal being conceded.

Four days later Jordan captained England at Wembley in a friendly with Spain. With two minutes to go England led 2-0 with Hendo having provided the cross for the second goal scored by Jamie Vardy but the shine was taken off the skipper's night as goals from Aspas and Isco brought Spain level.

That though was to be Jordan's last international for nine and a half months. Injury the following February ruled him out of the four internationals in the spring and summer but he was back at the start of September, captaining England for World Cup qualifying wins over Malta and Slovakia.

The following month Jordan remained in the side but without the armband as England were skippered by Tottenham's Harry Kane who scored the winners in 1-0 wins over Slovenia and Lithuania. While Henderson would captain the country twice more later in the season in wins over the Netherlands in Amsterdam and Costa Rica at Leeds Kane would become the first choice captain. Kane is an excellent player, a great goal-scorer and a solid character. Given that forwards rarely make good skippers and that he doesn't captain his club side there are those who think that playing for a London club and having the capital's media behind him contributed to the decision to have Harry rather than Hendo captaining England. To be fair to Southgate he is a strong, independently minded leader but with Hendo now having the experience of captaining his club to the European, World and Premier titles -and being renowned for his ability to drive his team on – it seems increasingly strange that he does not also captain the country.

So often England's performances at the finals of major tournaments have been fearful, safety first affairs. This cautious approach tends to have been the case despite England frequently going into competitions with an outstanding record in qualifying games before the fear factor stifles them on the big stage. Not so under Southgate in Russia at the 2018 World Cup. Fielding a young and vibrantly attacking team the waist-coated one gave his side licence to attack.

Hendo was at the heart of the park as Tunisia were tamed 2-1 and Panama paralysed 6-1, Jordan even taking the armband as captain Kane was subbed after completing his hat-trick just past the hour mark. With England through to the knock-out stages with a game to spare both Henderson and Kane were amongst those rested as Belgium inflicted a 1-0 defeat in Kalingrad.

This left England with a tricky Round of 16 match with Columbia. Kane's penalty looked likely to take England into the quarter-finals only for future Evertonian Yerry Mina to take the game into extra time with an added time header. With no further scoring the tie went to penalties. England's tournament record at shoot-outs did not instil confidence and neither did Henderson's. Rarely a penalty taker but now a senior member of the side he stepped up to take England's third spot-kick. All five up to now had been converted so a failure would mean a likely exit.

Standing stock still and weighing up his options Jordan looked focussed but not confident. He hit the penalty with power and it was well placed, low to Arsenal keeper David Ospina's left only for the goalkeeper to reach it and save it. Crestfallen, Henderson had no desperate show of emotion but he knew the odds were now stacked against his side. Unlike his manager however, who missed a key penalty in the Euro 96 semi-final against Germany, Jordan's penalty would be forgotten rather than leading to a subsequent pizza advert.

He was helped by another Jordan. A goalkeeper who was following him through the Sunderland Academy four years behind Hendo's age group and like him now plying his trade on Merseyside, albeit on the other side of Stanley Park. Jordan Pickford. After Mateus Uribe hit the bar and Kieran Trippier levelled, Pickford athletically thwarted Carlos Bacca's penalty to leave Eric Dier to keep his cool, slot home his spot kick and wonder of wonders enter England as shoot out winners at a World Cup!

Four days later Dier got a taste of the quarter-final he'd taken England to when he came on for Hendo with five minutes left as England protected a 2-0 lead against Sweden. A further four days on Dier would again replace Henderson but not in such happy circumstances. Taking on Croatia in England's first semi-final since Italia 90 England had started well. Trippier's brilliant free-kick had provided an early lead which Kane came close to doubling only to hit the woodwork from close range. An equaliser from Inter's Ivan Perisic mid-way through the second half tipped the balance as England laboured. Seven minutes into extra-time Southgate again made the Henderson-Dier switch but to no avail as four minutes into the second period of added time Mario Mandzukic of Juventus half-volleyed the winner for Croatia. This time it had not been Italy that ended Hendo's England hopes but players from Italian clubs had done the damage. Jordan sat out the third place play-off where England lost to Belgium before the squad returned to a nation where they were now heroes rather than scapegoats.

For the next year Jordan appeared in every game for which he was available. A 50th cap came as Jordan came off the bench in Montenegro. He marked the occasion by providing the killer pass for the final goal for Raheem Sterling as England won 5-1. Having come on as sub, Jordan had taken over the captaincy for the last few minutes when Kane was replaced, although Jordan also picked up a yellow card after a heated late exchange with Nikola Vukcevic.

Further yellow cards later in the year against the Czech Republic and Bulgaria led to him being suspended for England's show-piece 1000th international in

November 2019 on the ninth anniversary of his England debut but nonetheless 2019 further emphasised his value to the national side. By now this understanding was not just of the four England managers who have selected him but the fans who voted Hendo England's Player of the Year for 2019.

"It's a huge testament to what he's had to endure. I say that because obviously he had massive boots to fill when Steven [Gerrard] left. Jordan took the armband" commented Phil Babb who played for all three of the clubs Jordan has represented and starred at the 1994 World Cup for the Republic of Ireland. Speaking on Sky Sports Babb continued, "He has become a vital cog in the England machine. For fans to appreciate that shows you how well he's developed in the past few years. He's a supreme athlete, lives his life the right way. He's a good leader, he's tenacious and makes the right decisions."

In the summer of 2020 as Henderson lifted the Premier League title for Liverpool in the strangely prolonged season he should have been playing for England in the Euro finals. That will now take place in 2021 when he will hope to add international honours to his array of club and individual trophies. Clearly the Jordan Henderson story has several chapters still to be added.

## CHAPTER ELEVEN

# THE FUTURE

So what happens next for Jordan Henderson? Having filled his trophy cabinet to bursting between the summers of 2019 and 2020 there could well be many more playing honours to come. Having always looked after himself and always been tee-total there is no reason to believe he cannot continue to play at the top level for several more seasons. When the time comes that he can no longer command a regular place in the Liverpool team there will be no shortage of good clubs wanting to offer him a contract.

Perhaps he might fancy experiencing life abroad for a year or two although having a young family might lessen the appeal of that. Wherever former managers of his are employed when the time comes for Jordan to leave Anfield they are likely to be eager to sign him. Maybe he might be drawn back to his home town of Sunderland, perhaps stepping into a player-manager role.

Jordan may not fancy the managerial route but he appears to have the credentials to become a manager if he wishes. A student of the game renowned for putting the team first and seeing the bigger picture at all times he has gained the respect of fellow professionals throughout the game and is rightly seen as a strong character of considerable integrity.

Leadership qualities have been on display as he has led Liverpool to triumph after triumph while his initiative in sparking and sustaining the #PlayersTogether scheme during the Coronavirus pandemic demonstrated his ability to bring people together.

Having always been helpful to the media a post-playing career as a highly decorated pundit could be another option and it does not take a leap of imagination to see him succeeding Gary Lineker as a host of shows such as Match of the Day rather than simply being a talking head to be asked an opinion.

With plans to build a seven bedroom Cheshire mansion featuring a leisure suite, and most appropriately a trophy corridor, Hendo seems happy to see his long term future base being somewhere safe to bring his young children up. Whatever the future for Jordan professionally, his wife Rebecca and family will be centre to his world. From the time when Jordan was as young as his kids are now he has been dedicated to make himself a success.

Having reached the very top of the most cut-throat of self-centred businesses without making any known enemies Jordan has achieved all he set out to. He has earned the respect of both his fellow professionals and fans from across the country and beyond, not simply supporters of his own club. Throughout his journey he has stayed loyal to family and friends. As a teenager on loan with Coventry Jordan looked to the future and said, "Football is my life – it has been since I was a little boy. It's all I've ever wanted to do so I am prepared to give up everything I've got to become a footballer – whether that's leaving home or leaving my friends. My number one priority is football. I've dreamt of this since I can remember and I have never wanted to do anything else."

Jordan now has the game's top medals to his name, in excess of over 50 caps, some gained as captain of his country, and a deserved reputation as one of the top good guys in the game. He is the ideal role model, not just for any would be footballer but for anyone in any walk of life who wants to make their dream come true without selling their soul.

# APPENDIX

# HENDO IN NUMBERS

## LIVERPOOL*

| | APPEARANCES | GOALS |
|---|---|---|
| PREMIER LEAGUE | 229+40 | 26 |
| FA CUP | 13+5 | 0 |
| LEAGUE CUP | 19+3 | 1 |
| EUROPE & WORLD | 51+4 | 2 |
| **TOTAL** | **312+52** | **29** |

**To end of season 2019-20*

## COVENTRY CITY (LOAN)

| | APPEARANCES | GOALS |
|---|---|---|
| LEAGUE ONE | 9+1 | 1 |
| FA CUP | 3 | 0 |
| LEAGUE CUP | 0 | 0 |
| **TOTAL** | **12+1** | **1** |

## SUNDERLAND

| | APPEARANCES | GOALS |
|---|---|---|
| PREMIER LEAGUE | 60+11 | 4 |
| FA CUP | 2+1 | 0 |
| LEAGUE CUP | 5 | 1 |
| **TOTAL** | **67+12** | **5** |

## CLUB TOTALS*

| | APPEARANCES | GOALS |
|---|---|---|
| PREMIER LEAGUE | 289+51 | 30 |
| LEAGUE ONE | 9+1 | 1 |
| FA CUP | 18+6 | 0 |
| LEAGUE CUP | 24+3 | 2 |
| EUROPE & WORLD | 51+4 | 2 |
| **TOTAL** | **391+65** | **35** |

**To end of season 2019-20*

## ENGLAND*

| | APPEARANCES | GOALS |
|---|---|---|
| WORLD CUP FINALS | 7 | 0 |
| WORLD CUP QUALIFIERS | 8 | 0 |
| EUROPEAN CHAMPIONSHIP FINALS | 1+2 | 0 |
| EUROPEAN CHAMPIONSHIP QUALIFIERS | 11+1 | 0 |
| NATIONS CUP FINALS | 0+1 | 0 |
| NATIONS CUP QUALIFIERS | 2+0 | 0 |
| FRIENDLIES | 12+10 | 0 |
| **TOTAL** | **41+14** | **0** |

**To end of season 2019-20*